What Life Was Like ®

AT THE REBIRTH OF GENIUS

Renaissance Italy
AD 1400 ~ 1550

What Life Was Like

AT THE REBIRTH OF GENIUS

Renaissance Italy
AD 1400 - 1550

BY THE EDITORS OF TIME-LIFE BOOKS, ALEXANDRIA, VIRGINIA

CONTENTS

AT THE REBIRTH
OF GENIUS

COMING INTO THE LIGHT

Knowing even then that they lived in extraordinary times, 15th-century intellectuals named their own age—calling it the Renaissance, or "rebirth." And indeed, as Italy rediscovered the treasures of its ancient past, the beauty of the classical world *was* reborn. Inspired by crumbling architectural ruins, ageless sculpture, and Roman and Greek literature and learning preserved in ancient manuscripts, Italian scholars, artists, and architects unleashed a cultural tide that would engulf a Europe poised to break free from its medieval moorings and enter the modern age.

The classical world to which these Renaissance men looked for inspiration had been eclipsed by the barbarian invasions of Rome in the fifth century AD. With the dissolution of the Roman Empire, the political unity of Italy had vanished and, in the view of succeeding generations, the country had sunk into a 1,000-year period of provincialism, vulgarity, and ignorance. Later historians would refer to this period as the Middle Ages. The scholars of 15th-century Italy used a more dismissive term: They called it the Dark Ages.

In the centuries after the fall of Rome, some Italian cities evolved into sovereign states, absorbing smaller towns and dominating the economic and political life of the surrounding region. By the beginning of the 14th century, Venice, Genoa, and Flor-

1462	1465	1469	1471	1475-1564	1478	1484
Platonic Academy is founded in Florence	First Italian printing press is set up at Subiaco near Rome	Lorenzo de' Medici assumes power in Florence	Sixtus IV elected pope	Life of Michelangelo Buonarroti	Pazzi conspiracy against Medici; Spanish Inquisition begins	Innocent VIII elected pope

ence had populations of around 100,000. (Paris, by comparison, had about 80,000 inhabitants, and London about 40,000.) Free from the domination of kings or territorial princes, these and smaller city-states like Siena and Lucca developed into republics governed by committees of citizens. Others were autocracies—Ferrara, Milan, and Mantua, for example; one was a kingdom—Naples; and one an elected monarchy—the papacy in Rome. All were fiercely independent, constantly seeking ways to acquire more power and territory at the expense of their neighbors. And all possessed that one thing that made patronage of artistic and intellectual endeavor possible: wealth.

Strategically located in the great trading arena of the Mediterranean basin, Italy was a natural gateway between East and West. The coastal cities of Genoa, Pisa, and Venice had grown prosperous through trade with the Near East. Inland cities such as Florence and Milan became important export and banking centers to the rest of Italy and beyond. Independent, wealthy, cosmopolitan, and competitive, the city-states provided the ideal setting for a rebirth of culture and achievement.

Following the lead of Florentine poets Dante and Petrarch, scholars began to look to the art and ideas of antiquity, seeking out Latin and Greek manuscripts hidden in monasteries and for-

1486

Pico della Mirandola writes *Oration, on the Dignity of Man*

1492

Alexander VI (Rodrigo Borgia) elected pope; Columbus's first voyage across the Atlantic

1494

Charles VIII of France invades Italy

1498

Savonarola is executed; Leonardo da Vinci completes *The Last Supper*

1499

Louis XII of France invades Italy

1499-1503

Rise and fall of Cesare Borgia, son of Pope Alexander VI

1502

The Spanish conquer Naples

eign libraries. Interest in the classical world soon spread beyond literature to other disciplines—to sculpture and architecture, for example, and to music and science. And a new philosophy based on classical ideas emerged: Called humanism, it eschewed the medieval focus on God and theology. According to the humanists, many of whom were devout Christians, there could be only one starting point for intellectual reasoning: *studia humanitatis,* the study of humans and their capabilities.

Nowhere was this cultural blossoming more spectacular than in Florence—Firenze, "the city of flowers." Established in 59 BC as a Roman colony on a narrow stretch of the Arno River, Florence had by the 15th century come to dominate the province of Tuscany and much of central Italy. It was also home to a dazzling array of geniuses: sculptors Donatello and Michelangelo; architects Brunelleschi and Alberti; writer Machiavelli; painters Masaccio and Botticelli; and the universal genius, Leonardo da Vinci. And not least, Florence was home to the merchant banking family of the Medici, who for three generations were the foremost patrons of art and humanist learning during the Renaissance. "Now, indeed, may every thoughtful spirit thank God that it has been permitted to him to be born in this new age," declared the Florentine humanist Matteo Palmieri in the 1430s, "so full of hope and promise, which already rejoices in a greater array of nobly-gifted souls than the world has seen in the thousand years that have preceded it." This conjunction of genius and prosperity produced an unparalleled outpouring of creativity, and

1503	1508-1512	1513	1517	1521	1523	1527
Alexander VI dies; Julius II elected pope	Michelangelo paints the Sistine ceiling	Leo X (Giovanni de' Medici) elected pope; Machiavelli writes *The Prince*	Martin Luther posts his 95 theses	Magellan's ships circumnavigate the world	Clement VII (Giulio de' Medici) elected pope	Rome is sacked by troops of the Holy Roman Empire

Florence—which was the only large Italian city with no significant classical remains—was transformed into one of the world's most glorious civilizations.

The Renaissance marked a transition from the medieval to the modern for the city-states. They went from a world in which the economy was based on agriculture and where intellectual inquiry was based on religious teachings to a world of growing national and political consciousness, of commerce and capitalism, of increasing secular control of areas previously the exclusive domain of the church.

The same period that witnessed Italy's cultural triumph also saw the country's political disaster. Machiavelli had warned that the disjointed and ever-warring states would have to unite if they were to remain independent and strong. But factionalism in the peninsula was deep seated. The city-states had grown used to competition and rivalry. When covetous French, German, and Spanish armies turned their attentions to their wealthy neighbor, Italy could do little to resist.

By the early 16th century, the Renaissance in Italy had reached its peak, and its influence was spreading to the rest of the Continent, evident in the work of Erasmus and Dürer, Sir Thomas More and Shakespeare, Cervantes and Montaigne. And as mighty European armies marched south into the peninsula, Italians might have taken some consolation from the knowledge that the powerful ideas and attitudes of their Renaissance were moving just as surely north.

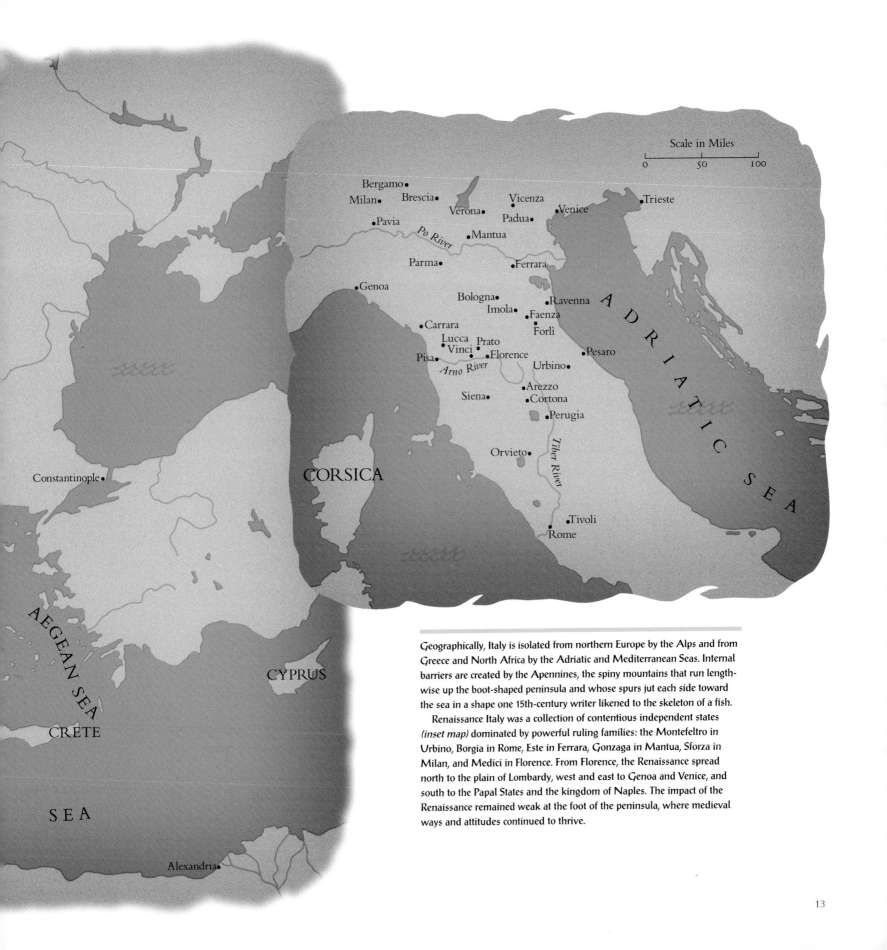

Bergamo •
Milan •
Brescia •
Verona •
Vicenza •
Padua •
Venice •
Trieste •
Pavia •
Po River
Mantua •
Parma •
Ferrara •
Genoa •
Bologna •
Imola •
Ravenna •
Faenza •
Forlì •
Carrara •
Lucca •
Prato •
Vinci •
Florence •
Pisa •
Arno River
Urbino •
Pesaro •
Arezzo •
Siena •
Cortona •
Perugia •
Orvieto •
Tiber River
Tivoli •
Rome •

CORSICA

A D R I A T I C   S E A

Constantinople •

CYPRUS

AEGEAN SEA

CRETE

S E A

Alexandria •

Scale in Miles
0   50   100

Geographically, Italy is isolated from northern Europe by the Alps and from Greece and North Africa by the Adriatic and Mediterranean Seas. Internal barriers are created by the Apennines, the spiny mountains that run length-wise up the boot-shaped peninsula and whose spurs jut each side toward the sea in a shape one 15th-century writer likened to the skeleton of a fish.

Renaissance Italy was a collection of contentious independent states *(inset map)* dominated by powerful ruling families: the Montefeltro in Urbino, Borgia in Rome, Este in Ferrara, Gonzaga in Mantua, Sforza in Milan, and Medici in Florence. From Florence, the Renaissance spread north to the plain of Lombardy, west and east to Genoa and Venice, and south to the Papal States and the kingdom of Naples. The impact of the Renaissance remained weak at the foot of the peninsula, where medieval ways and attitudes continued to thrive.

13

THE FIRST FAMILIES OF RENAISSANCE ITALY

As the Renaissance dawned, Italy was a patchwork of small independent city-states. Governmental committees dominated by a few aristocratic families held sway in Venice, Genoa, and Florence; the papal court ruled Rome; and princely families reigned over territories controlled by the Holy Roman Emperor and the Papal States.

While Florence and Venice were seen as great cities, the city-states of Mantua, Ferrara, Urbino, and Milan also sponsored some of the most significant intellectual and artistic accomplishments of the 15th century. In Mantua, for example, Gianfrancesco I Gonzaga invited humanist scholar Vittorino da Feltre to open what came to be called his school of princes, which counted among its graduates military leaders and patrons of the arts. Milan's court commissioned paintings by Leonardo da Vinci, and in Ferrara, Ercole I put together a choir to rival the Vatican's.

The ruling families gained their wealth and political influence from trade and banking, from industry, by hiring out their armies, and in the case of the Borgias of Rome, by having a patriarch as pope. Strategic alliances between the clans were forged not only through military partnerships but also through arranged marriages. By the close of the 15th century, most of Italy's first families were closely intertwined by marriage and political and economic interdependence.

Federigo da Montefeltro, shown here in military dress, commissioned this portrait of himself and his son, Guidobaldo, upon receiving the title of duke of Urbino from the pope. In his private study *(inset)*, Federigo read and worked surrounded by trompe l'oeil depictions of landscapes, buildings, and weapons.

URBINO AND THE LIGHT OF ITALY

Federigo da Montefeltro, duke of Urbino, made his fortune as Renaissance Italy's most respected and highly paid condottiere, or military general for hire. He is known to history, however, for the way he spent his riches—transforming his tiny duchy into one of the cultural centers of Europe.

The son of the ninth count of Montefeltro, whose family had ruled the region for 300 years, Federigo received a classical education under Vittorino da Feltre in neighboring Mantua. There he studied mathematics, music, and Latin, learned to dance and to ride, and developed an appreciation for the arts. As Federigo later observed, he was instructed "in all human excellence."

The young noble also studied warfare and was soon in demand as a military leader. His reputation for fairness and diplomacy helped him gain the support of Urbino's citizens when his half brother, the count of Urbino, was assassinated in 1444. As the new ruler, Federigo used his own income to lower taxes, help the poor, open schools and medical centers, and store emergency grain. "So kind was he," wrote historian Vespasiano da Bisticci, "that they all loved him as children love their parents."

Federigo spent even more of his considerable wealth to acquire art and to build a grand palace. In addition, he "maintained a fine choir with skilled musicians and many singing boys," observed Vespasiano. But books were Federigo's passion, and he wished to create the finest library since ancient times. He employed 30 copyists and illuminators, who produced a library second in size only to the Vatican's. His silver- and gold-inscribed manuscripts included classics in Greek, Latin, and Hebrew, along with a deluxe edition of Dante's *Divine Comedy* and a Bible bound in gold brocade.

Federigo's cultural legacy continued with his son, Guidobaldo. Guidobaldo and his wife, Elisabetta Gonzaga of Mantua, gathered around them a brilliant circle of intellectuals and artists, including painter Raphael and writer and diplomat Baldassare Castiglione, who memorialized Federigo as "the light of Italy."

Battista Sforza, daughter of Alessandro Sforza of Pesaro, married Federigo in 1460, at the age of 14. She died of pneumonia six months after the birth of their ninth child—and only son—Guidobaldo.

Alexander VI, in his bejeweled papal vestments, kneels in adoration of Christ in this detail from Pinturicchio's *The Resurrection.* To those Romans who resented the idea of a Spanish pope, Alexander's death from malaria at age 72 was cause for much rejoicing.

Cesare Borgia *(right)* was feared and hated by many, but he also served as the inspiration for *The Prince,* by Niccolò Machiavelli, who called him "truly splendid and magnificent." Cesare seized much of central Italy using armaments designed by his engineer, Leonardo da Vinci.

THE BORGIAS IN ROME

Two of her three marriages—all arranged by her father—ended badly for Lucrezia Borgia. Following her marriage to Duke Alfonso d'Este of Ferrara, she devoted herself to good works.

"A man of an intellect capable of anything," historian Iacopo da Volterra noted favorably of Spanish-born Vatican official Rodrigo Borgia in 1486. By the time Borgia's 11-year reign as Pope Alexander VI ended in 1503, many in the church's inner circles agreed with him—but for different reasons.

Borgia's uncle, Pope Calixtus III, brought his nephew into the church in 1456, when Rodrigo was only 25 years old. Distinguishing himself as cardinal and then vice-chancellor of the Vatican, Borgia was named pope in 1492—an election likely eased by promises of cash payments and lucrative jobs to those who supported him.

The new pope accomplished much during his reign: He rebuilt the University of Rome, refilled Vatican coffers, and set about regaining control of the Papal States, which had fallen under the rule of local dictators. With the shrewdness of a statesman—but ignoring Christian principles—Alexander financed this campaign by appropriating the estates of deceased bishops and selling divorces to Europe's kings and princes.

The pope's son Cesare—he fathered at least nine illegitimate children, whom he openly acknowledged—led the papal armies into battle. A ruthless leader, Cesare imprisoned and executed those who resisted, and he employed treachery when force failed. In 1502 his troops overran Urbino only weeks after Guidobaldo da Montefeltro, Urbino's duke, had lent the Vatican army his artillery.

Alexander put at least 30 other relatives on the church payroll, and once appointed his daughter Lucrezia to handle Vatican business while he was away. Unsavory rumors circulated about Lucrezia and her father and brother—incest, treachery, poisonings, and violent murder—but while she was certainly a pawn in her family's political maneuvers, there was never any evidence of improper behavior on her part.

Ferrara's Duke Ercole I *(right)* possessed a somewhat icy demeanor and was quickly dubbed North Wind by his subjects. His attitude softened, however, upon his marriage to Eleonora of Aragon *(above)*. Well educated and much admired by her subjects, Eleonora—shown here receiving a wand from a celestial hand—was considered by some to be a more able administrator than her husband.

FERRARA: PEACE AND PRESTIGE

This 1499 woodcut of Ferrara is dominated by the city's wide Boulevard of Angels, part of which was reserved for promenading courtiers—the "angels." Such scenes of life among the nobility, including a detail of court musicians *(right)*, were depicted in murals by Francesco del Cossa.

The city-state of Ferrara, strategically located along the trade route between Bologna and Venice, had one of the most prosperous and peaceful courts of the Renaissance. Although Ferrara technically belonged to the papacy, the Este family ruled as independent lords. During the reign of Niccolò III, the domain reached its greatest extent, having Rovigo, Modena, Parma, Reggio, and—for a brief time—Milan within its borders. Niccolò reduced taxes, encouraged business, and established a highly regarded school. And in 1438 he welcomed a council of scholars and prelates whose meeting served to heal the schism between the eastern and western branches of the Catholic Church.

Three of Niccolò's sons—he sired more than 30 children in all—reigned in turn. Leonello, the eldest, was a master of Greek, Latin, philosophy, and law and was avidly interested in humanism and the arts. He established public libraries and endowed the university, drawing to Ferrara outstanding scholars from across Europe. Leonello shunned opulence—unlike his brother Borso, who succeeded him in 1450. Borso taxed his citizens heavily, and he spent a good deal of the proceeds on elaborate musicals, pageants, dances, and plays and on works commissioned from poets Ludovico Ariosto and Tito Vespasiano Strozzi and artists Cosimo Tura and Francesco del Cossa. Described by Pius II as a garrulous man who "listened to himself talking as if he pleased himself more than his hearers," Borso's grandiose ways brought acclaim to Ferrara—and also brought the title of duke to Borso.

Ercole I, the last of Niccolò's sons to reign, was a devout man who so loved sacred music that he recruited a chapel choir to rival the Vatican's. He too patronized the arts, but perhaps his most dramatic contribution was the extension of the city, called the Herculean Addition. Its homes, palaces, churches, convents, and defensive structures tripled Ferrara's size and made it the most modern city in Europe.

In this scene from Andrea Mantegna's fresco series in Mantua's ducal palace, three generations of Gonzagas gather at the outskirts of the city. Francesco *(center),* named a cardinal in 1461, is greeted by his father, Ludovico *(left).* The two boys in the foreground are Francesco's nephews, the future cardinal Sigismondo *(left)* and Francesco II, the future marquess and husband of Isabella d'Este.

MANTUA'S SCHOOL OF PRINCES

Francesco II Gonzaga, shown here in his general's uniform, was taken prisoner by the Venetians in 1509. After his release—which was secured by his wife, Isabella—Francesco fell ill with syphilis. Isabella ruled until his death 10 years later.

The Gonzaga family, rulers of Mantua for four centuries, were known for their harmonious court, their military cunning, and their guardianship of a reliquary said to contain drops of Christ's blood. But their most enduring contribution was the founding of a school headed by scholar Vittorino da Feltre.

Invited to Mantua in 1425 by Marquess Gianfrancesco I, Vittorino instructed the children of noble families in subjects ranging from athletics, military arts, and mathematics to painting, music, and religion. Mantua was soon deluged with requests that students from other cities might attend the "school of princes."

The education of Ludovico, the marquess's eldest son, served Mantua well. Later, as a successful general-for-hire, he had ample resources for patronage. He commissioned architect Leon Battista Alberti to design and build the churches San Sebastiano and Sant'Andrea, and he brought to Mantua the painter Andrea Mantegna.

Ludovico's passion for the arts was shared by Isabella d'Este, wife of his grandson, Francesco II. Isabella collected rare books and was one of the first noble patrons to acquire artwork solely because of the artist rather than the subject matter.

In matters of state, Francesco was more soldier than politician, and he depended increasingly on Isabella. Though not born into the family, Isabella was perhaps the most remarkable Gonzaga of the 15th century, and her shrewdness played a pivotal role in defending the interests of her adopted home.

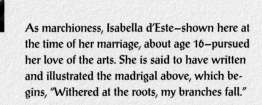

As marchioness, Isabella d'Este—shown here at the time of her marriage, about age 16—pursued her love of the arts. She is said to have written and illustrated the madrigal above, which begins, "Withered at the roots, my branches fall."

MILAN: WEALTHY AND STRONG

Milan hummed with industry under the rule of the Visconti family. In 1423, revenues from the manufacture of armaments and fine cloth brought in 12 million gold florins—an income more than that of either Venice or Florence. But in 1450 the dynasty ended when Duke Filippo Maria Visconti, the last of his line, died without an heir. Into his place stepped Francesco Sforza, a young mercenary general married to Visconti's illegitimate daughter.

Francesco—a man "with a combination of bodily and intellectual gifts unrivalled in our time," as Pius II put it—broadened the reach of Milan's industry and trade and cut a network of canals to irrigate vast new farmlands. He built the city's Great Hospital, completed its cathedral, and brought humanist scholars to court. Under his rule, Milan became northern Italy's leading military power.

When Francesco died in 1466, he was succeeded by his oldest son, Galeazzo. Unlike his father, Galeazzo was known for his cruelty and debauchery, which led to his murder. Since Galeazzo's heir was just a child, Francesco's other son, Ludovico, ruled as regent.

Nicknamed Il Moro for his dark, Moorish looks, Ludovico brought even greater prosperity to Milan, including the development of an experimental farm and cattle breeding station. A man with many mistresses, Ludovico finally, at age 39, wed young Beatrice d'Este. Beatrice's appetite for luxury was insatiable. Shortly after her wedding, she ordered 84 satin gowns embroidered with gold and studded with gems. She also had Leonardo da Vinci create mechanical devices and mathematical puzzles to amuse the court.

Just a few years into the marriage, Ludovico began an affair with a beautiful courtier. The pregnant Beatrice tried to ignore the betrayal, and one evening, after dancing late into the night at a ball, she fell ill. She gave birth to a stillborn son, and several hours later she died, at age 22.

Racked with guilt, Ludovico never recovered. Soon after, Italy was invaded by France, and Milan was lost. Il Moro died in a French dungeon in 1508.

To ensure his loyalty to her father, mercenary general Francesco Sforza *(top)* was married to Bianca Maria Visconti *(bottom)*, daughter of the duke of Milan. When the duke died without an heir six years later, Sforza gained control of the dukedom.

Kneeling opposite each other, Ludovico Sforza and his wife, Beatrice, present their two young sons to the Virgin and child *(right)*. Beatrice died in 1497, following the birth of her third child. Ludovico's fondness for lovely women included Cecilia Gallerani, depicted below in *Lady with an Ermine* by Leonardo da Vinci. A poet, patron of the arts, and the duke's mistress, Cecilia was living in the palace when Ludovico brought his young bride home in 1491.

CHAPTER ONE

RENAISSANCE WOMEN

Although portraits were a popular form of Renaissance painting, Fra Filippo Lippi's *Portrait of a Man and a Woman at a Casement* is unusual in that the couple is shown in a domestic setting. Given the woman's prominence and elaborate costume, the work may have been commissioned to mark a special event, such as a marriage or the birth of a male heir.

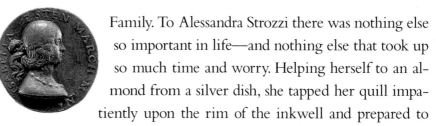

Family. To Alessandra Strozzi there was nothing else so important in life—and nothing else that took up so much time and worry. Helping herself to an almond from a silver dish, she tapped her quill impatiently upon the rim of the inkwell and prepared to write to Filippo, her eldest son. Things would be so much simpler, she sighed, if her three grown-up sons had remained here in Florence at their widowed mother's side. But Filippo and his youngest brother, Matteo—now in his early 20s but still, in Alessandra's heart of hearts, her baby—were in Naples, working in the bank and textile warehouse Filippo had established there. Lorenzo, Alessandra's middle son, was in the Flemish city of Bruges, another outpost of the far-flung trading empire of the Strozzi.

Alessandra, born into one merchant house and married into another, wouldn't have felt so bitter if her sons had simply been away on business. But politics, rather than commerce, kept them far from home. For it was their misfortune to belong to a clan of Florentine patricians that was almost, but not quite, as powerful as the mighty Medici. And not only were the Strozzi influential, but they stood on the wrong side of the political divide.

Tailors cut and measure cloth to make garments like those hanging on the beam above them in this shop scene dated about 1500. Florentine woolens were the finest in Europe; their production supported a large part of the population in and around the city, from rich capitalists and merchants to low-paid spinners, carders, and dyers.

For the span of a generation or more, there had been little love lost between the rival houses. Back in 1434, when the Medici faction took control of the city, they had banished any members of the Strozzi family who might pose a threat to their regime. Alessandra's husband, Matteo, had fallen victim to the purge. With seven young children in tow, she followed him to his place of exile in Pesaro, on the Adriatic Sea. Barely a year after their move to that marshy and, she thought, unwholesome coastal region, Matteo and three of their offspring died of plague. At the time Alessandra was pregnant again, carrying the male child who would be christened with his dead father's name.

It was neither legally required nor customary for an exiled man's wife and children to suffer under the same ban. So after Matteo's death, Alessandra brought her surviving brood back to Florence. But the Medici had a long and vengeful memory. A few weeks before Alessandra sat down to write this letter, the state had imposed a sentence of banishment on her two eldest sons. Filippo and Lorenzo were now grown men, who scarcely remembered the father in whose name they suffered so unjustly.

This winter afternoon in early 1459 found Alessandra in an irritable mood. She always disliked the month of February, when mists rolled off the Arno River and dampness oozed through the narrow streets of Florence. The very act of letter writing, even to Filippo, fatigued her. Nevertheless, as she so often reminded her children, she never shirked a sacred duty, be it attendance at Mass or the composition of missives bearing domestic news, reports on family finances, and motherly advice. She dispensed these in the simple penmanship she'd learned at her mother's knee. Her handwriting may not have displayed the elegance of the script that young male patricians acquired from their humanist tutors, but the recipients of her letters had no trouble understanding every word.

She took another almond from the dish and bent again to her task of consoling Filippo.

"It's been a comfort to me, seeing you've taken what has happened as well as you possibly could. You've made the right decision, because there's nothing we can do about it."

The situation, she continued, could have been far worse. In fact, she had just received some encouraging news from the authorities. The exiles would henceforth be allowed to come somewhat closer to Florentine territory. "They've reduced the limits to 50 miles." Even better, she was now permitted to correspond with her sons without first showing the official censors every letter sent or received.

Still, she would warn Filippo not to let his guard down when

Weavers, who operated out of their own homes, bought or rented looms like this early-16th-century model in exchange for regular payments of finished work.

29

he wrote. "I think my letters are being treated the same way yours are and I seldom get one which hasn't been opened. I don't know who's doing this." She didn't need to spell out the obvious truth—the regime would always mistrust an exile's connections back home. "So don't write anything important to me unless it comes by someone trustworthy and I'll do the same."

As always, she felt obliged to remind her son Filippo to work hard and show respect to his employer, the Strozzi cousin who had some years earlier taken the fatherless boy under his wing and taught him everything a successful businessman needed to know. "You should consider your position and think what Niccolò has done for you and be worthy to kiss the ground he walks on. And I say this out of love for you, because you have a greater obligation to him than to your father or mother."

Alessandra, although she wouldn't dream of saying this aloud, believed that cousin Niccolò was also under an obligation to Filippo. According to the morals of the day, a deceased man's closest relatives should, as a point of honor, see to the upbringing of his orphaned sons.

Merchant-banker Filippo Strozzi *(right)* exceeded his mother's expectations for him in business, becoming a very wealthy man. He built his financial empire in Naples after the Strozzi family was banished from Florence in 1434 by their powerful rivals, the Medici.

Alessandra herself was no great reader, but she would have appreciated the sentiments of one of her Florentine contemporaries, the humanist Leon Battista Alberti, who, in his *Book of the Family,* enjoined the kinsmen of fatherless youths "to help these boys to become good men, and to do for their education and guidance what you would want done for your own children in case of need."

But not every family was blessed with such honorable men. If the Strozzi cousins hadn't taken their responsibilities to heart, Matteo's widow and orphans might have found themselves in desperate financial straits. It would have been unthinkable for Alessandra, as a woman of the patrician class, to take up any form of paid employment. Luckily, she had inherited some country properties from her husband; the tenants' rents and the sale of wine from these estates provided her with an income. She spent most of it on her sons.

She refrained from reminding her children how fortunate they were to have such a devoted mother. Alessandra had lost her husband when she was only 28 years old; many young widows would have remarried. But she had no wish to see the progeny of her first marriage reduced to the status of stepchildren in another man's house. For the sake of Filippo and his brothers, she chose the life of a Strozzi widow instead of a stranger's wife.

Ever conscious of her duties,

Alessandra kept a hawklike eye on the family's finances. As befitted the daughter of a mercantile family, she was as numerate as any of her male relatives, capable of calculating profit, loss, and interest, and no stranger to the intricacies of double-entry bookkeeping.

As she pictured her son perusing the ledgers in his Neapolitan counting house, Alessandra allowed herself a rueful smile. In his youth Filippo had displayed a feckless streak; she'd dispatched more than one letter chiding him for his profligacy: "From all I hear you know more about throwing money away than about saving a penny." But now, she reflected, making the sign of the cross and murmuring a prayer of thanks to heaven, he'd apparently mended his ways.

Then she turned her attention to more mundane matters, such as his chronic indi-

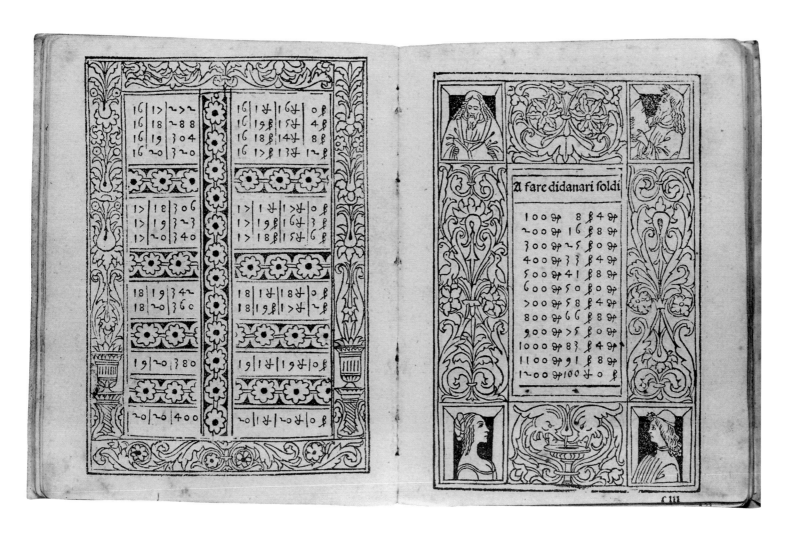

This decorative arithmetic primer was used by merchants and tradesmen in their everyday business calculations; multiplication tables are on the left, and at right is a table for converting Florentine coins. Sons of the merchant class usually received hands-on business training at age 13, after traditional schooling in grammar, geometry, and Latin.

gestion. "I'll send you the jar of aromatic herbs, but the best medicine for your stomach is to watch what you put in your mouth!"

Reaching out for another almond, she remembered how her son had sent her a sackful of these nuts from Naples, along with three jars of sweetmeats, a large supply of capers to add zest to the household's dinners, and 36 pounds of flax for her to spin into linen thread. "It's good of you to remember me," she had written him, "because these days I need your kind thoughts, but I'd like to have you near me even more."

The shipment had arrived in a wicker cart, in the care of a courier named Favilla. In Naples, Favilla had gotten a cash deposit from Filippo, but at the Strozzi house in Florence he demanded more. Alessandra, who knew Favilla well, didn't quibble, but she reported the transaction to her son just to keep the record straight. "He asked me to give him 4 soldi straight away because he needed the money, and to pay 3 lire and 2 soldi later, so I did. I've credited the 3 lire and 2 soldi which I didn't pay to his account."

This talk of money reminded Alessandra that she had some urgent business to attend to. It was time to put down her pen. She closed her letter with a promise and a pious wish—"I'll keep you informed about everything. Nothing more for now; remember us to Niccolò and do look after Matteo. May God keep you from all harm. From your Alessandra in Florence."

She wrapped herself in a thick woolen cloak against the dankness of the day and set off with weary tread to pay her taxes. The state, always hungry for revenue, was squeezing patrician families hard. She had almost worn out a pair of shoes trudging from one gloomy government office to another in her campaign to get the tax assessment reduced. Today a payment was due.

The errand was a sharp reminder of her family's woes. Ladies of her class made few public appearances, apart from their walks, with downcast eyes and a phalanx of chaperons, to Mass. If only, thought Alessandra, her husband were still alive or her sons at home! They would have been the ones marching out to negotiate with blank-faced bureaucrats in the palaces of state, while she stayed happily indoors with her needlework, sheltered behind the walls of the family mansion.

Making her way through the city's crowded streets, she did enjoy one small consolation. It was always interesting to see what other women were wearing. She took comfort in the fact that nobody else's cloak looked as well cut as her own. The Strozzi were prominent members of the wool-merchants guild; it was a point of honor for her to maintain the appropriate sartorial standards.

Alessandra herself had been born into the Macinghi family, a less distinguished, although still patrician, lineage; they were prominent residents in the district surrounding the church of Santa Maria Novella. Her relatives had rightly regarded Alessandra's match with Matteo Strozzi as a coup, cementing a useful political alliance and raising their own social status in the city.

Now the years had flown by, and Alessandra—as the middle-aged mother of five grown-up sons and daughters—found few things in life quite as intriguing as the making of marriages. Indeed, when the bubonic plague made one of its periodic visitations, reaping a terrible harvest, one of Alessandra's first reactions was to lament, "The plague's a great inconvenience for girls because hardly any marriages are being arranged here."

In matrimonial matters, a patrician woman had just two roles. When young, she was required only to act the obedient bride, passively handed over to whatever young man suited her family's dynastic purposes. Later in life, she would inevitably take an interest in finding spouses for her children. But even then, she played her part discreetly. Marriages were decided—if only officially—by the man of the house. And all but the most rebellious of sons would defer to paternal wisdom when taking a wife. The family's economic and social interests took precedence over any sentimental inclinations.

Girls married as early as 14 years of age. By age 18, a woman not yet betrothed or wed would feel that life had passed her by.

AT HOME IN A RENAISSANCE CITY

Built in the mid-14th century, the Palazzo Davanzati was typical of homes owned by the wealthy families of Florence. Tall, narrow, and dimly lit, the house extends well back from the Via Porta Rossa and retains some of the fortified aspects of its architectural forebear, the medieval tower. In contrast to its rather grim facade, however, the interior of the Palazzo Davanzati was lavishly decorated and furnished, filled with the antiquities and art that befitted the home of a Florentine aristocrat.

As in other such homes, the ground level of the Palazzo Davanzati served as a storehouse for produce from the family's country properties; had Davanzati been a merchant, this floor would also have housed his place of business. An inner courtyard with a well admitted light and air to the interior rooms. Beginning with the patriarch's apartments on the second floor, each successive level provided a complete living space for the family's sons, who continued to live in the home even after marriage. The spacious top-floor loggia was the crowning glory of the Palazzo Davanzati: On this covered balcony one could take in fresh air as well as magnificent views of the city and the Tuscan countryside.

The first-floor stronghold of the Palazzo Davanzati lends a fortresslike appearance to the townhouse. The family coat of arms is prominently displayed on the building's sandstone facade.

The second-floor grand salon, part of the family patriarch's living space, was located at the front of the house, directly overlooking the street. All family events and entertainments—such as banquets and receptions—would have taken place in this spacious and elegantly appointed room.

Located on an upper floor to prevent smoke and cooking odors from permeating the entire house, the kitchen was equipped with cooking hearth, preparation tables, and various utensils. It also contained equipment for other domestic activities, such as spinning, weaving, and sewing.

Adjoining the grand salon, the dining room, also known as the Room of the Parrots, was decorated with bird-motif trompe l'oeil frescoes that were designed to look like tapestry hangings.

One of the bedrooms at the rear of the house still possesses its period furnishings and wall decorations. Adjacent antechambers contained toilets that emptied down chutes.

In that case, she might find that the only option left to her was to enter a convent and live out her days as a nun. A young man, however, was free to sow his wild oats well into his 30s, until parental pressure drove him to the altar.

Back in 1447 Alessandra had found a fine husband for her older daughter, Caterina. The bride was 16 at the time of the wedding; her spouse, Marco Parenti, was 25. Both families congratulated themselves for doing well out of the match. The bridegroom's lineage wasn't nearly as ancient or exalted as Caterina's. But—thanks to the Strozzi's current political and economic woes—her family was willing to look kindly on someone who, in happier times, might have been considered beneath her.

Alessandra had only good things to say about her son-in-law. He was, as she'd purred in a letter to Filippo at the time of the betrothal, a "worthy and virtuous young man, and he is the only son, and rich." He owned a silk factory, and his father had recently served a term in the city government, so they were not entirely nonentities.

Fortunately the Parenti had agreed to accept the modest sum of 1,000 florins

This gilded storage chest, or cassone, was designed and decorated with a tournament scene by Apollonio di Giovanni, a partner in one of Florence's busiest art workshops. Cassoni held trousseaux of clothing, jewelry, silver, and cloth and were often commissioned by a bride's father as part of her dowry. The chests, measuring anywhere from three to eight feet long, occupied a prominent place in Renaissance decor.

as a dowry—500 in cash and movable goods, handed over on the day of the marriage, the remainder to come from money that had been invested on Caterina's behalf in the state dowry fund, payable later. To buy a groom from a nobler house, Alessandra would have had to spend at least half again as much, and that wouldn't necessarily have guaranteed her daughter's happiness.

Marco, to Alessandra's relief—and doubtless to Caterina's—seemed besotted with his young bride. He lavished dazzling gifts upon her. Alessandra's mouth watered as she thought of them: a crimson velvet gown made up from silk woven in Marco's own workshop—"the most beautiful cloth in Florence"; another gown, rose colored this time and pearl embroidered; an elaborate headdress, crafted in the form of a garland, adorned with the finest feathers and dripping with pearls. All this, said Marco, was no more than Caterina deserved, since she was, in his eyes, the loveliest girl in the city.

Alessandra prayed for the newlyweds' happiness. But sentimentality had its limits. When, shortly after the wedding, Caterina became pregnant, her mother's first thought was of the half of the dowry still sitting in the state fund. What if, as Alessandra delicately stated, "God has other plans" for Caterina? In a letter to Filippo she discussed the financial risks attendant on a death in pregnancy or childbirth: "I think we should take out some insurance so we won't lose the five hundred florins they're owed from the Fund, as we could lose her and the money at the same time."

Alessandra even broached the subject of a short-term insurance policy with her son-in-law, who thought it an unnecessary expense. The mother-to-be seemed in excellent health. But Alessandra decided that it was up to the Strozzi, not to Caterina's husband, if they wanted to protect their investment. So she went ahead and purchased the policy without telling Marco Parenti. As an additional form of insurance, she prayed fervently and frequently that Caterina come through the pregnancy "healthy in body and soul."

As custom dictated, men and women sit separately at a marriage feast painted by Sandro Botticelli, though the groom visits with the bride at left, offering her wine. Despite sumptuary laws regulating excessive wedding expenses, the wealthy still spent lavishly to publicize their new alliances. Indeed, marriages were so politically important in Florence that the Medici monitored most nuptial contracts, including the one between the Pucci and Bini families commemorated here.

Her prayers were answered. In February 1450 Caterina bore a son. Despite their disagreement about life insurance for Caterina, Marco enjoyed a good rapport with his mother-in-law. For the rest of her days, he would help her manage her affairs, serving almost as a surrogate son in her own boys' absence.

Alessandra also liked Giovanni di Donato Bonsi, who married her second daughter, Lessandra, in 1451. Bonsi was, she reported to Filippo, "a respectable, well-behaved young man, and quite acceptable; he has so many good qualities." But despite his many virtues—and his willingness to accept a dowry worth only 1,000 florins, in cash and goods—Giovanni's business acumen did not match his manners.

He and Lessandra eventually found themselves so hard up that they had to come and live in Alessandra Strozzi's house. After her husband's debts spiraled beyond control, Lessandra put a brave face on things. When she couldn't afford to replace a ragged underskirt, she covered it with a loose, flowing gown, in hopes that nobody would notice the tatters underneath.

Alessandra wrote to Filippo that her son-in-law "doesn't say much about his own business, but I know he sometimes pawns the few clothes he has and hides the fact from me because he is ashamed." She and Marco Parenti tried hard to help Giovanni get back on his feet.

However great her concern for her daughters, Alessandra—reflecting the attitudes of her time—invested far more emotion in her sons. When her youngest boy, Matteo, left home to begin his commercial education under Filippo's tutelage, Alessandra did not suffer in silence: "I don't know how I can live without him, because I feel so unhappy and love him too much because he's just like his father."

Greater pain would follow for Alessandra Strozzi. In August 1459 word came from Naples that her precious Matteo had died of malaria—or, possibly, of plague. Shaken to the core, Alessandra found consolation in religion. Her faith was uncomplicated and

THE FRUITS OF MARRIAGE

A new mother lies in bed while matrons care for her swaddled infant and female visitors are ushered in by two nuns on this 15th-century birth tray, made to commemorate the arrival of a male heir.

Announced by a herald, male kin—who were not allowed to enter the room—bring gifts, like this tray of sweets. Patrician women were richly re-warded for producing sons, thought their primary purpose. Yet children were not always cause for joy: No trays were commissioned for girls, and one in 10 Florentine women died giving birth.

strong. She went regularly to Mass not simply for the sake of an excursion, but because she knew it would save her from hell's torments.

Like most Florentines, Alessandra venerated relics and holy pictures, celebrated the feasts of certain saints with a cultist's zeal, and scrupulously adhered to the rules of the Lenten fast even when she was sick. She encouraged her sons to perform charitable acts for the sake of their immortal souls, convinced that a friend's swift recovery from illness was heaven's reward for his good deeds.

Her own soul, she believed, could do with some extra protection. She had even considered making a pilgrimage to Rome, to gain a papal indulgence that would wipe her slate clean of sins. She had tried to persuade Filippo to travel up from Naples and meet her, since the holy city lay halfway between them, but her plans for the reunion never bore fruit.

Among Florence's rich panoply of churches, she had her particular favorites. She often made her way to Santissima Annunziata, which contained an altar where bereaved relatives placed wax images of their departed loved ones. And, while praying for Matteo in heaven and her two older sons on earth, Alessandra would scrutinize the girls of good family waiting their turn at the confessional or lighting candles at a shrine. Perhaps among them she would find the perfect spouses for Filippo and Lorenzo.

Her sons were well into their middle and late 30s, more than ripe for matrimony. And she had made her feelings plain: "If all men were so afraid of getting married," she wrote in 1465, "the world would be empty by now!"

This remark was slightly disingenuous, since Lorenzo had already contributed to the human population by fathering several

illegitimate children. Alessandra remained sanguine about such liaisons; boys would be boys, and her son's behavior didn't differ from that of any other young patrician male. But children born on the wrong side of the blanket didn't count.

Now she felt it was time for Lorenzo to put aside his current mistress, and well past time for Filippo to sever his long attachment with Marina, his slave-girl concubine. Her sons owed it to her, and to the entire family, to make honorable marriages worthy of the House of Strozzi.

On this particular day no nubile maidens of the parish—apart from one whose awkward gait, coarse complexion, and poor dress sense made her an unlikely candidate for the very discriminating Filippo—had chosen to pray at Santissima Annunziata. So Alessandra decided to continue her devotions at the cathedral.

Arriving just in time for Mass, she congratulated herself on her good fortune. Peering into the perpetual twilight of the nave, she spotted a young lady in a blue velvet dress, absorbed in her prayers. Alessandra sat down beside her and spent the duration of the Mass discreetly scrutinizing the young woman's appearance and general demeanor. Did she look robust enough for childbearing, while still elegant enough to bespeak good breeding? Did she seem intelligent—yet not so cocksure that she would challenge the word of husband or mother-in-law?

Afterward, following her quarry out into the piazza, Alessandra had to laugh at her own folly. The stranger who had intrigued her in the dimly lighted church turned out—in broad daylight—

to be the Tanagli girl, already under consideration as a possible bride for Filippo. Alessandra's son-in-law Marco had broached the subject with the Tanagli, who didn't seem entirely hostile to the idea. But negotiations had hardly begun, and the family might have second thoughts about handing over their daughter to an exiled and out-of-favor Strozzi.

She had already warned Filippo that, once a good candidate came along, he should snap her up. There weren't many fathers willing to ally themselves with such a troubled house, unless they were too poor to offer a decent dowry or were trying to dispose of a daughter who had something wrong with her. Unfortunately, Filippo dithered too long and lost the Tanagli girl to a more avid suitor.

Alessandra remained undaunted. She had also heard good reports about a young lady from the Adimari family. To get a closer look at her, she found out what churches the girl attended and determined the streets and squares she was likely to pass through on her infrequent outings. But, as she reported to Filippo, "I've gone to all the places and she hasn't been there as she usually is." When she finally caught up with the maiden four months later, she liked what she saw. "Buy the Adimari girl," she advised Filippo. "She's good meat with lots of flavor."

Filippo took his mother's advice and married Fiammetta Adimari after his exile ended in 1466. It marked a turning point. Not only did Filippo ally himself with a maiden of good family, but he also made peace with the House of Medici. He launched himself into the business of finding a wife for his younger brother—and made it clear that the only acceptable candidates for the match would be from families approved by Piero de' Medici himself.

To set a seal on the reconciliation, in 1469 Filippo's wife was invited to the wedding celebrations for Piero's son Lorenzo and Clarice Orsini. The festivities would last for days. At the time Fiammetta was pregnant. Pleading her delicate condition, she sent her regrets. But the bridegroom's mother, Monna Lucrezia, wife of the all-powerful Piero, would not brook any refusal. Morning sickness or not, Filippo Strozzi's lady was wanted at the feast. Alessandra basked in the reflected glory.

Alessandra soon had her own grounds for celebration. The baby that Fiammetta bore Filippo was a healthy boy, who was named Alfonso. Alessandra prized this new arrival far more highly than any grandchild produced by a mere daughter, since only a son's son could perpetuate the family line.

To ensure the safety of the Strozzi's posterity, the happy grandmother took considerable interest in the choice of a wet nurse. Few middle-class or aristocratic mothers

Despite efforts at urban renewal dating from the end of the 13th century, the streets of Renaissance Florence remained a narrow and winding network running between rows of closely packed houses and shops, as seen in this painting by Francesco Ubertini. These streets were the preserve of men.

Well-to-do women stayed home, especially marriageable girls, whose chastity was so closely guarded that they were, according to one resident, "seldom seen either at the window or at the door." If they had to go out, chaperons accompanied them to ensure propriety. Lower-class women, on the other hand, such as the two carrying bundles at the far right, went about their errands more freely.

This glazed terra-cotta medallion of a swaddled infant is one of many that adorn the facade of Filippo Brunelleschi's Ospedale degli Innocenti *(bottom)*, a famous foundling home of 15th-century Florence.

CHARITY FOR THOSE IN NEED

Beginning in medieval times, the care of the sick and the feeding of the poor were religious duties performed by members of the church. Indeed, many monastic orders, like the Franciscans, had been founded for that very purpose. During the 15th and 16th centuries, however, the challenges posed by a rising population throughout Italy were too great for the church alone to meet. As a result, many cities built hospitals, almshouses, and foundling homes, and lay organizations as well as individuals began to take responsibility for some of the roles that had once been the preserve of the church.

Florence was particularly well en-dowed with institutions set up to tend to the needs of the poor, the sick, and the unwanted. In the 15th century the city boasted 35 hospitals run by public and private donations. And as early as 1421 the first foundling home was endowed there by the silk-manufacturers guild. The Ospedale degli Innocenti, as it was known, was a place where orphaned children were cared for through the charity of the merchant guilds. Designed by the renowned architect Filippo Brunelleschi, the foundling home exemplified the fine workmanship that often went into such institutions, expressions in stone and mortar of the importance with which the Renaissance world regarded good works.

A frieze on the Ospedale del Ceppo at Pistoia, near Florence, depicts one of the traditional seven works of mercy, feeding the hungry.

A detail from a Florentine chapel fresco from around 1480 portrays the annual distribution of cloth to the poor by the powerful wool-manufacturers guild.

45

nursed their own babies. The Tuscan countryside was well supplied with lactating peasant women whose own infants had died or who were willing to suckle a small paying guest alongside a baby of their own. Many upper-class Florentine children, farmed out to cottagers, became acquainted with their parents only when they returned to the family home around the age of two.

This system of child rearing at a distance had its perils. Alessandra made sure to alert her son and daughter-in-law to the tales she'd heard of careless wet nurses who had fallen asleep and crushed the infants lying beside them, of callous creatures who let their charges sicken or starve. But Alessandra stood vigilant guard over the welfare of her brood; when little Alfonso suffered from any childhood ailment, she monitored every rash and sniffle.

Alessandra argued with Filippo about the

zled by the early-morning sun. She nodded a greeting to her next-door neighbor Tita Cavicciuli, who was busy sweeping the threshold of her husband's silk-weaving workshop.

Then, swinging an empty basket and humming an old love song, Lusanna set off down the street. A moment later, alerted by a sudden rumbling, she pressed herself against a wall. A farm cart trundled past, laden with artichokes, heads of fennel, and two old women holding wicker cages crammed with clucking chickens. Lusanna caught them staring at her; one whispered something to the other and both laughed, exposing thick toothless gums.

As the cart moved off, her eyes met those of the man who stood on the opposite side of the street. He gave her a barely perceptible nod, then smiled. She felt her face flush, averted her eyes, and stepped into the stream of people heading toward the market.

"Buy the Adimari girl. She's good meat with lots of flavor."

choice of names. She felt unhappy when Filippo deviated from contemporary custom and refused to name a son Matteo, in memory of her husband. Nevertheless, the son she had once chided about mending his ways had, at the end of the day, made his widowed mother very happy. Filippo restored the family to its place of honor in the Florentine establishment, succeeded brilliantly in his business ventures, and built a massive palace that would, 500 years later, remain as one of the city's most imposing landmarks, proclaiming the magnificence of the House of Strozzi.

From another, much less grand house in Florence, on the Via San Gallo, emerged Lusanna di Benedetto, wife of the linenmaker Andrea Nucci. She paused for a moment in the doorway, daz-

Lusanna didn't need to look back. She could feel her pursuer's gaze sweeping back and forth across her shoulder blades, gliding down her back, and tracing the sway of her hips. She quickened her pace, glanced over her shoulder. He was still there, though keeping a discreet distance between them.

At this hour, when Florence geared itself up for another day of buying and selling, the streets were always crowded. Today, for some reason, the crush seemed worse than usual. She sidestepped a packhorse struggling under bales of wool and almost collided with an apprentice steering a handcart into the apothecary's shop.

Then she reached the cause of the congestion: Two black-clad scholars, engrossed in philosophical debate, stood facing each other, as oblivious as rocks in a river to the human current flowing around them. So heated was their argument that neither noticed the pickpocket sidling ever closer to them. Lusanna saw the quick flick of a little blade, as a deft movement separated a leather purse from the belt where it had dangled. If she cried a warning, the victim might yet catch the thief in the act. But, not wanting to draw attention to herself, she held her peace and hurried by. As she passed the mansion newly built by one of the richest men in the quarter, she nearly collided with a little procession emerging from its portals. A pale matron, flanked by two elderly chaperons and followed by a Tartar slave girl carrying a little cushioned stool, sallied forth to morning Mass at the Church of San Lorenzo. Lusanna wondered whether she should envy the lady her protectors or pity her for her lack of freedom. She cast a quick glance up the street. Her follower hovered, awaiting her next move.

She slipped off the thoroughfare and began threading her way through a warren of alleyways, some of them so narrow that she had to negotiate them sideways. After a time, she paused, looked back, and waited. There was no one behind her.

Emerging into the bustle of the Old Market, the Mercato Vecchio, Lusanna became absorbed in the quest for something to tempt her ailing husband's appetite. She moved quickly past the tables of the moneychangers and headed for the fishmongers' stalls.

She contemplated a bucketful of writhing eels and looked for signs of life among the baskets of crayfish. A tray of red mullet, though artfully displayed, she rejected as not quite fresh enough. Then, as Lusanna turned away, she felt someone take her by the elbow.

"Giovanni," she muttered through clenched teeth. "I thought I'd shaken you off."

Whatever words passed between them next were exchanged in whispers. Lusanna had her reputation to think of. She was a married woman. As an artisan's wife, she might sometimes find it necessary—in the course of business—to speak to a man who was not a member of her family. But a conversation in the mar-

ketplace was risky. What would her neighbors think? Still, it was difficult not to feel flattered when pursued, to the point of obsession, by a handsome young patrician who called her the most beautiful woman in Florence and vowed that he would someday make her his own.

Even if she hadn't already possessed a husband, Lusanna would have had good reason to doubt Giovanni's word. They lived in the same neighborhood, heard Mass at the same churches, and confessed to the same priests, but they still moved in very different social circles. Lusanna was a tailor's daughter and a linenmaker's wife. Giovanni della Casa was a worldly and well-traveled merchant prince whose commercial interests extended from international banking to the silk trade. His family was on excellent terms with the Medici.

But several months later, in January 1453, Giovanni found his opportunity. Lusanna's husband died. Lusanna did what was proper for a widow with no children of her own: She moved in with her married brother, Antonio, and his wife. Giovanni, excited and hopeful, began patrolling the street outside their house.

Antonio, outraged by this slur on his family's honor, tried to persuade the importunate suitor to go away. He appealed to Lusanna, who merely shrugged her shoulders. It would be scandalous for her to speak outright to Giovanni. What did Antonio expect her to do?

Finally Antonio confronted Giovanni. If he wanted Lusanna, he would have to marry her, to "give her a ring." Giovanni, to Antonio's relief, agreed. Lusanna, like any conventional Florentine woman, stood back and let her closest male relative conduct the negotiations on her behalf.

But this would not be a conventional alliance. For a start, Giovanni made it clear that he did not require any dowry. He may well have charmed his prospective brother-in-law by declaring that Lusanna's beauty was prize enough for him. However, Giovanni did lay down one condition: The marriage had to be kept secret, for fear that his father would disinherit him for taking a bride from a class so much lower than his own. Surely Antonio would understand.

Florentine wedding ceremonies were normally conducted under the supervision of a notary. Giovanni explained that this would be impossible. His father, Lodovico della Casa, was one of the most influential men in the neighborhood. What lowly notary would dare to risk della Casa's wrath by officiating at his son's clandestine marriage? None of them could be trusted. The very mention of such a match would send them scuttling off to Ser Lodovico, eager to ingratiate themselves by revealing the truth.

Antonio may have felt uneasy, but he eventually agreed, as long as the marriage was sanctified by the presence of a priest. Giovanni suggested a trustworthy cleric, Fra Felice Asini, a Franciscan friar at the convent of Santa Croce. Both Antonio and his sister were satisfied.

On a warm May evening Fra Felice and a young novice arrived at Antonio's house to find a festive dinner party in progress. Around the table sat the prospective bride and groom; Antonio and his wife, Cosa; Antonio and Lusanna's stepmother, Mea; and a married couple, Giuliana and Niccolò Magaldi, who were friends of Antonio's and business acquaintances of Giovanni's. A

At this "ring-day" ceremony, a notary records the couple's agreement to the union arranged by their fathers or other male kin.

Away from the avid eyes of city gossips, the couple felt free to let their guard down. They ambled hand in hand under the blue Tuscan skies, picking flowers or gathering salad greens for supper. There were occasional excursions—to a neighbor's house to celebrate a baby's birth, and to the monastery of Vallombrosa. With Giovanni at her side, Lusanna saw no need to don her widow's weeds and instead dressed in a light brown tunic, such as any married woman of her age might wear.

At one point during this rural idyll, Lusanna realized she'd been wearing Giovanni's wedding ring for weeks on end and now couldn't pry it off her finger. This, she reminded Giovanni, could be dangerous; she had promised him never to wear it in public. What would happen if she still had it on her hand when they returned to Florence? Giovanni surprised and delighted her when he replied resolutely, "It is well that it be known."

But once back in Florence, in the shadow of his father's house, Giovanni seemed to lose this bravado. Secrecy reigned once more. Lusanna had no choice but to accept it. Then, in February 1455, came the news that Ser Lodovico della Casa had died. Lusanna, feeling only slightly guilty about her gladness at an old man's passing, couldn't help but rejoice. Now she and Giovanni could live openly as man and wife.

Giovanni had an unpleasant surprise in store for her, however. His father's death, rather than releasing him from this double life, had apparently jolted him into a recognition of his responsibilities as scion of a great merchant house. In April of that year, with all the public pomp and ceremony expected of a Florentine patrician, he married the 15-year-old daughter of Piero di Cardinale Rucellai, whose family was even more exalted than Giovanni's own.

When she heard the news, Lusanna was devastated. Her shock and bewilderment soon gave way to righteous wrath: "That traitor Giovanni has deceived me!" she roared to her neighbor Monna Fiora. "I am his wife!" When she calmed down, her first instinct was to try and win him back again. She persuaded various friends and neighbors to visit Giovanni and act as go-betweens. And she made sure he knew that other men—respectable citizens—had proposed to her, through marriage brokers, and that she had turned them down. Giovanni was her husband; what need had she of suitors?

Then Lusanna stunned everybody, especially Giovanni, by taking him to court. As a mere woman, she wasn't able to bring the suit herself, so her brother, Antonio, as her legal guardian, initiated the proceedings on her behalf. She declared that Giovanni's marriage to Marietta Rucellai was bigamous and petitioned the church to declare it null and void.

Giovanni responded through his lawyers. Yes, he had indulged in a longstanding relationship with Lusanna. Indeed, he stated that their liaison dated back to 1443, 10 years before her husband's death. But this union had been nothing more than an adulterous affair. If Lusanna claimed it was a lawful marriage she was either daydreaming or lying.

The citizens of Florence saw nothing strange in a liaison between a male patrician and a woman from a lower social class. These things happened all the time. Although young men of good family—like Alessandra Strozzi's sons—stayed single until well into their 30s, no one expected them to live like monks.

Officially, adultery violated the laws of both church and state, but prosecutions were rare. An aristocrat might find himself in trouble if he dallied with the unwed daughter of a patrician house; the scandal would debase her value in the marriage market, and his crime could be viewed as a form of theft. Nuns, of course, were also strictly off-limits.

Even in the days when his passion for Lusanna blazed most fiercely, Giovanni had managed to beget two illegitimate sons elsewhere. On his tax declaration for the year 1458 he would include Carlo and Marco, born in 1453 and 1455 respectively, among his dependents.

These two little boys, sons of an unidentified mother or mothers, were luckier than most. For every father who, like Giovanni, took responsibility for the unofficial twigs on his family tree, there were hundreds who did not. The city's orphanages and foundling hospitals were full of infants abandoned by women who had themselves been deserted by their paramours.

According to Lusanna's friends, she herself had contemplated adopting a baby from one of these institutions. Her marriage with Andrea Nucci had been childless. She frequently visited the church of Santissima Annunziata, where she prayed to an image of the Annunciation that was believed to cure infertility in women.

This yearning for a child may have been one of the reasons that she responded to Giovanni's advances. His lawyers, however, based

The hearings began at the end of June. But they had barely got under way when Antoninus learned that Lusanna was now the subject of a police investigation. Some unnamed person had denounced her to the city's chief magistrate, the podesta, accusing her of murder. It was alleged that her late husband, Andrea Nucci, had not—whatever his physician believed—died of natural causes. Lusanna had deliberately poisoned him.

The archbishop thought the timing of this allegation just a little too convenient to be plausible. A simultaneous murder investigation could only damage Lusanna's chances of a fair hearing in her prosecution of Giovanni. He politely requested the podesta, Giovanni della Porta, to call a temporary halt to his own investigations. Once the church had reached its verdict, della Porta

"*Whatever else she deposed is not true and so she revokes it.*"

their case on the grounds that Lusanna was a promiscuous woman, whose word was as worthless as her morals were weak. If anyone had made the first immoral advances, it was not Giovanni but the woman who now dragged him into court.

The case was conducted in the religious courts, under the supervision of Antoninus, archbishop of Florence. He was an expert in ecclesiastical law, having served many years in the high court of the Papal Curia. But Antoninus had come from humble beginnings, growing up in the same narrow streets as Lusanna herself. Neither wealth nor power nor an ancient pedigree impressed him. The archbishop had little love for patricians who exploited the poor and considered themselves exempt from the laws of God and man. "The Church," he declared, "supports the small and the weak."

would be free to press ahead with the police case. In his view, the religious courts took precedence over the secular.

The podesta refused. He knew that powerful patricians—Giovanni's own family, his new Rucellai in-laws, and possibly, the Medici themselves—wanted Lusanna discredited. Antoninus responded by issuing a writ of excommunication. The podesta, perhaps fearing the Medici more than he feared eternal damnation, stood firm. Finally the city fathers intervened. Deciding that the scandal of an excommunicated chief magistrate was too terrible to contemplate, they ordered him to yield to Antoninus. With this hindrance removed, the archbishop and his aides set to work.

Lusanna's witnesses included the friar who had performed the wedding ceremony; the peasants who'd seen her with Giovanni during their rural idyll; her stepmother, Mea; and Cosa, her brother's wife. They testified that she was a virtuous widow who had entered into marriage with Giovanni in good faith.

Giovanni's lawyers scorned these protestations. They announced to the court that this selfsame Fra Felice Asini had at one time been sentenced "as an infamous friar and malefactor" to a ceremony of public humiliation in the city of Cortona. How could such a man's testimony be trusted? And it had been well known throughout the parish of San Lorenzo that Lusanna played her husband false. Indeed, some wag once nailed a set of horns—the ancient symbol of cuckoldry—to Andrea Nucci's door on the Via San Gallo.

Even the Cavicciuli, Lusanna's old San Gallo neighbors, joined the parade of hostile witnesses. They recounted rumors about her loose morals and remarked upon her brazen habit of returning men's glances when she passed them in the streets, instead of modestly lowering her eyes. Prompted by Giovanni's lawyers— and perhaps by their resentment of her aspiration to marry into a higher class—Lusanna's one-time friends now reported that she had borrowed their bedrooms for illicit encounters, even while her husband lived.

Some of the most damning evidence came from Giuliana Magaldi, who had shared Lusanna's wedding supper and had watched the exchange of rings. But Giuliana now denied that she and her husband, Niccolò, had ever eaten any such meal or witnessed any nuptial rites. All she would admit was that she had once heard Giovanni agree to take Lusanna for his wife if her husband should die.

Then Giuliana Magaldi came out with an even more shocking piece of evidence. She had met Lusanna soon after Andrea Nucci's death. The supposedly grieving widow had boasted about contaminating Nucci's food with some kind of silver powder and had said to Giuliana, "So tell *that* to Giovanni!"

As the hearings—and the summer—dragged on, the atmosphere grew ever more poisonous. Antoninus and his assistants

An ornate tabernacle at Santissima Annunziata in Florence housed an image of the Virgin reputedly painted by an angel. The painting was particularly venerated by women trying to become pregnant.

weighed the reams of contradictory evidence and assessed the motives of those who testified.

The archbishop knew that Lusanna's detractors were also Giovanni's economic dependents—wives of artisans employed at his silk factory, humble folk whose proudest boast was that the noble Giovanni della Casa had stood godfather to their children. Yet those of Lusanna's relatives who spoke on her behalf also had their own agenda: the protection of their family's honor at all costs. Somebody somewhere had to be lying.

And somebody was. On September 29 Antoninus and his chaplain took Giuliana Magaldi to the church of San Salvatore and questioned her, under oath, about her earlier testimony. Perhaps she was awed by the sacred precincts in which this interrogation took place; perhaps she had suffered some sleepless nights since her first court appearance. But Giuliana suddenly changed her story. Only one part of her first statement was correct: She had indeed heard Giovanni vow to marry Lusanna if she were ever widowed. The rest, she now confessed, was sheer fabrication. The clerk recorded her declaration: "Whatever else she deposed is not true and so she revokes it."

The archbishop didn't take long to arrive at his verdict. Giovanni and Lusanna had indeed exchanged rings and promises in the presence of witnesses and with a cleric's blessing. They may not have followed the conventional procedure for contracting a marriage, but both parties had patently given their consent. Therefore Antoninus decreed that the match was lawful and the subsequent union with Marietta Rucellai null and void. Giovanni was now commanded to acknowledge Lusanna as his lawful wife and to treat her "with marital affection."

Lusanna felt vindicated. She and Giovanni had almost certainly been lovers for years before her husband's death, but that made no difference to the case's outcome. Giovanni could no longer spurn her.

Her joy would be short lived. Giovanni della Casa's family, thanks to their Medici connections, had a direct line of communication to Pope Calixtus III. A year after Archbishop Antoninus's verdict, the Papal Curia reversed his decision, declaring Lusanna's marriage invalid. Giovanni was free to resume his comfortable life with Marietta Rucellai. Nothing more was heard of Lusanna.

In the city of Verona, a young woman with other things besides marriage on her mind emerged from morning Mass in a throng of worshipers. The cathedral had seemed unusually full this morning, and in the crush 19-year-old Isotta Nogarola had somehow lost both her sister Ginevra and their elderly maid. Impatient to find them and head for home, she scanned the crowd. Suddenly she felt a light tap on her shoulder. She turned, expecting Ginevra, but found instead a semicircle of well-dressed young women, all struggling to keep straight faces.

"Still waiting for word from on high?" asked one.

"Don't despair, dear girl. Perhaps your very brilliance has simply struck the great man dumb."

"Can you tell us, oh learned Isotta, what is the Latin for 'well and truly snubbed'?"

Overcome by their own wit, the girls succumbed to a collective fit of giggles. Then they linked arms and sauntered away.

Isotta's cheeks blazed. She wished the paving stones of the piazza would part and let her sink into the earth. All Verona seemed to know that the highly educated Isotta Nogarola had committed an outrageous act—and all Verona knew that she had received a fitting comeuppance.

Isotta and her sister Ginevra belonged to a noble family with progressive ideas and a strong love of learning. Their parents, members of an atypical minority who believed that daughters deserved as good an education as sons, had hired a tutor named Martino Rizzoni. Rizzoni was a pupil of the great educator Guarino da Verona, a pioneer of the new approach to learning known as humanism. The humanist curriculum sought to

Renaissance tribunals, like the one above from the manu-script *De Sphaera*, operated much like modern-day courts. Although Florence's judicial system was among the best in Europe, it was administered by a confusing variety of criminal, civil, and church agencies, and their rulings could be arbitrary and were occasionally manipulated by the rich.

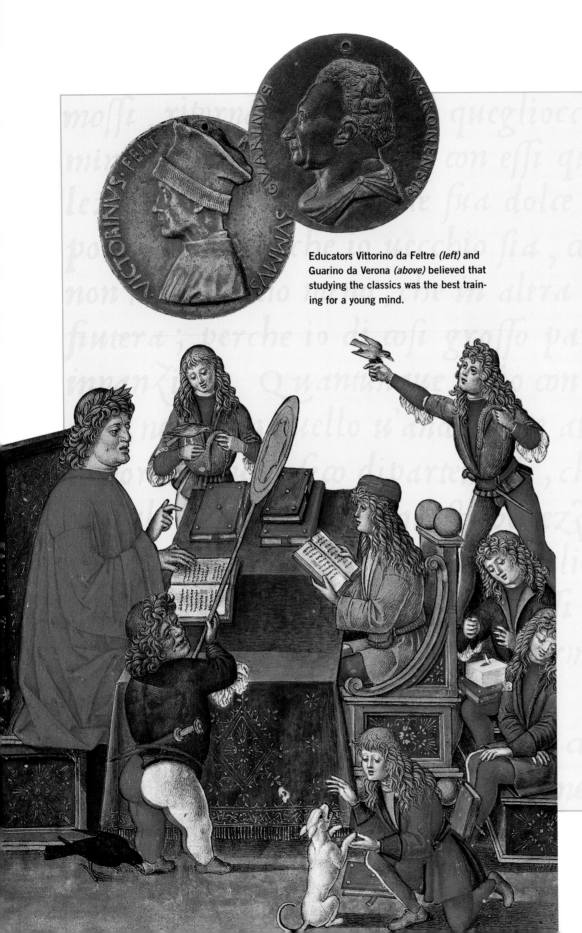

Educators Vittorino da Feltre *(left)* and Guarino da Verona *(above)* believed that studying the classics was the best training for a young mind.

A HUMANIST EDUCATION

While teachers in the Middle Ages had focused on memorizing and acquiring specific kinds of knowledge, humanist educators of the Renaissance saw learning in a different light. Inspired by classical Greece and Rome, humanists believed that the purpose of schooling was to produce men equipped to fit knowledgeably—and with charm—into any walk of life. For the most part, women were excluded, their education a matter to be taken care of at home.

In cities across Italy, humanists set up schools to give young men a classical education in poetry, grammar, rhetoric, history, and moral philosophy. The two most famous of these schools were those of Vittorino da Feltre in Mantua, and Guarino da Verona in Ferrara. Although originally intended for the sons of the princely rulers of Mantua and Ferrara—the Gonzaga and the Este—both schools later accepted gifted poorer boys as well as pupils from other parts of Italy.

Like children today, some Renaissance students were unmoved by the new approaches to education. When young Massimiliano Sforza, the future duke of Milan, was asked what he wanted most in life, his reply was simple: "Not to go to school."

This painting shows young Massimiliano Sforza imagining all of the fun he could be having if he didn't have to pay attention to his tutor.

endow the rising generation with eloquence, intellectual agility, and moral understanding.

Rizzoni's course of study for the Nogarola sisters included most of the key subjects on the humanist agenda. They received a thorough grounding in Latin and read the great works of the ancient Christian and pagan poets, historians, and philosophers. The only subject likely to have been neglected was rhetoric: Women had no need to study the art of oratory, since they were not expected—or permitted—to play any part in public life.

Isotta and Ginevra proved apt pupils. By their late teens, both had acquired a reputation for their intelligence. Examples of Isotta's eloquent prose had begun to circulate among the region's men of letters, and praise flowed in from as far afield as Venice and Ferrara. Isotta's talents, her admirers declared, far exceeded those of other women. But such well-meant words displeased her. She wanted to be assessed as a scholar pure and simple, not as that freak of nature—a mere woman who could actually think.

When a young man wished to make a name for himself as a humanist, the customary first step was to initiate an exchange of letters with some respected sage. If his correspondent paid him any compliments, he would make sure these endorsements were widely publicized. Isotta, desperate to enter the community of scholars on her own terms, had done the same thing. And she had set her sights high, writing to the leading humanist of the day, Guarino da Verona himself.

Word of Isotta's brazen act spread through the palaces and villas of upper-class Verona. The women of that social circle, contemptuous of her intellectual pretensions, seemed gleeful when she got her just deserts. For Isotta had written the letter to Guarino at the beginning of 1437; now the year was almost over, and the great man had not yet deigned to reply.

Stung by the sound of her persecutors' mocking laughter, Isotta gave up her search for Ginevra and the maid. She strode across the cathedral square in a furious temper and, ignoring her neighbors' disapproving glances, walked home alone. Once indoors, she marched straight to her writing desk, picked up her pen, and fired off a second letter to Guarino.

Isotta had framed her first missive in decorous terms, appropriate for addressing a silver-haired savant three times her age. This time she unleashed a howl of fury.

"There are already so many women in the world! Why then was I born a woman, to be scorned by men in words and deeds? I ask myself this question in solitude. I do not dare to ask it of you, who have made me the butt of everyone's jokes. Your unfairness in not writing to me has caused me such suffering, that there could be no greater suffering."

She told him how optimistic she had felt when she'd written that initial, unanswered letter. She reminded him that he had already given her encouragement, by singing her praises to mutual acquaintances: "You yourself had said that there was no goal I could not achieve. But now that nothing has turned out as it should have, my joy has given way to sorrow." She had become a laughingstock, and it was all his fault. "For they jeer at me throughout the city, the women mock me."

This time Guarino answered promptly.

"This evening your letter arrived, full of complaints and accusations." He made no excuses for his silence, but chided her instead for disappointing him: "I knew that your mind, adorned with knowledge, was excellent, yet up to now I believed and trusted that your soul was manly, and that brave and unvanquished you could face all adversities. But now you seem so humbled, so abject, and so truly a woman, that you demonstrate none of the estimable qualities I thought you possessed."

Having thus rubbed salt into the wound he had inflicted, Guarino may have repented slightly, for he followed up his dig at woman's weakness with a stirring call to battle: "Be joyful, gay, radiant, noble and firm; create a man within the woman!"

In the darker corners of the world of letters, however, lurked

The ascent of the hill of knowledge, seen in this 15th-century miniature, began at the gate of grammar. Scholars then pursued arithmetic, logic, music, astronomy, geometry, rhetoric, and theology.

those who claimed that an intellectual woman was not only unnatural but depraved. In 1438 an anonymous Veronese writer denounced Isotta on the grounds that "an eloquent woman is never chaste" and backed up the generalization with a string of salacious and highly personal slanders: "Before she made her body generally available for promiscuous intercourse, she had first permitted—and indeed even earnestly desired—that the seal of her virginity be broken by none other than her brother."

Although outraged, Isotta refused to let such bigotry break her spirit, and she persevered. She turned her back on Verona, with its wagging fingers and provincial attitudes, to settle in the sophisticated waterborne metropolis of Venice. It was the greatest maritime capital of the age, mistress of the rich flow of commerce between East and West. Those merchant princes who had waxed fat from its traffic in silks, spices, textiles, leather, jewels, and glass adorned its 117 islands and 150 canals with palaces and churches. And along with their trade in worldly goods came an equally lively trade in fresh ideas.

Stimulated by the change of scene, Isotta bent with even more fervor to her studies. Her fame increased. But the learned men who read her writings still insisted on comparing her only with other women. It was always her gender, not the merits of her arguments, that intrigued them.

In 1441 she returned to Verona, retired with her books to a secluded room in her brother's house, and gave up her humanist ambitions. Religion, she decided, was a safer subject for a woman. For the next 25 years she lived like a nun in a cell, devoting herself to the study of sacred letters.

A male humanist with Isotta's talents would never have had to make such a choice. There were plenty of opportunities for those who wished to carve out a career. A learned man could become a private tutor, helping to mold the minds of young princes and patricians. Heads of state needed secretaries fluent in Latin to conduct their diplomatic correspondence; rich patrons called upon philosophers to help plan the allegorical paintings and symbolic sculptures to decorate a library or family tomb.

None of these paths were open to Isotta or to the handful of women like her. Men might be fascinated by a young maiden with formidable intellectual gifts, but—like Cassandra Fedele, who dazzled the students and faculty of the University of Padua when she delivered an oration on the liberal arts—a grown-up female scholar was a far more threatening proposition.

The average patrician wanted a wife whose accomplishments would enhance the quality of life within his own four walls. Girls of good family were therefore expected to know how to read and write in their native tongue; the ability to quote a little Dante, scrutinize the household's account books, and do exquisite needle-work was also appreciated. But a good grasp of Roman rhetoric or Greek philosophy would have seemed not only superfluous, but—to most husbands—fairly alarming.

"Shall I marry, or devote my life to study?" the young humanist Alessandra Scala asked Cassandra Fedele.

"Do that for which your nature has suited you," was Cassandra's enigmatic reply.

Both women understood that marriage and its responsibilities would spell the death of their intellectual aspirations. And both—like Isotta's own sister Ginevra—married anyway and put aside their books. The one female humanist who sought to combine the roles of wife and scholar was Laura Cereta, from Brescia, and even she was able to dedicate herself fully to her studies only after her husband's death.

Women who had no desire either for romance or for children might enter a convent where scholarship was tolerated or even encouraged. But the monastic life did not guarantee intellectual freedom: A nun was always at the mercy of her mother superior and the authoritarian male hierarchy that ruled the church. Isotta, thanks to her family's wealth and goodwill, was free to create a celibate life that suited her own tastes and inclinations. Her

In a detail of a painting by Gentile Bellini, Cardinal Bessarion (above, left) presents a Byzantine reliquary of the true cross to representatives of Venice's church of the Carità. A renowned Greek scholar, Bessarion was an admirer of the writings of Isotta Nogarola.

room, set apart from the household's noise and bustle, was furnished with well-stocked bookshelves, religious pictures, sacred relics, and flasks of holy water. She dressed in simple garments embroidered with crosses and the images of saints, which, according to one visitor, made a striking contrast with "the golden robes and bursting wardrobes" of her female relatives.

In a silence broken only by the birdsong that drifted through her window, Isotta passed her days studying and writing. It was not an entirely reclusive life. She enjoyed the company of her mother and siblings and sometimes received visitors.

One frequent guest was a local schoolboy named Matteo Bosso, who grew up to become a canon. "I would go to you from play and from school and with you and with your noble and wise mother I would pass the time," he reminisced. "And I would sit also in your book-lined cell, where I joyfully heard you delightfully singing sweet hymns."

Isotta also sustained strong intellectual friendships, corresponding with aristocrats, humanist scholars, and senior churchmen such as Cardinal Bessarion and Ermolao Barbaro, bishop of Verona. But her deepest bond was with Ludovico Foscarini, Verona's Venetian governor. Foscarini—an illustrious humanist, lawyer, diplomat, and politician—shared Isotta's love of learning. In an extended series of letters, the two exchanged ideas, discussed their reading, and engaged in philosophical disputations.

Isotta, stimulated by these encounters, composed a dialogue in which she and Foscarini debated the relative guilt of Adam and Eve. In a series of inventive arguments, she sought to prove that Eve's was the lesser sin. Isotta might have been an exceptional woman, but not even her formidable intellect was strong enough to resist the prevailing prejudices of the age. So she based her defense of her sex on the shibboleth that woman was the weaker vessel and therefore less able than Adam to resist the devil's wiles. The work was much admired by her contemporaries and was regarded by later generations of scholars as a classic of its kind.

But her relationship with Foscarini was more than a mere meeting of like minds. During the years that Foscarini governed Verona, he visited the Nogarola house often, conversing far into the night with Isotta, her mother, and her brother Antonio.

Foscarini's relationship with Isotta remained platonic, but there were powerful emotional undercurrents. At one point the bishop of Verona—their mutual friend—requested that Foscarini curtail his visits, for fear they would distract Isotta from her pious meditations.

Isotta's male supporters took comfort in her nunlike seclusion from the world and her self-imposed vow of chastity. Sequestered inside this invisible cloister, her unfeminine intellectual acuity posed less of a threat. But Isotta may not have been entirely happy in this state of singleness. Her health began to break down, and she began to suffer from chronic pain in "stomach and body."

In 1453, at the age of 35, she received—and seriously considered—a proposal of marriage. She wrote to Foscarini for guidance. Should she accept? His reply was unequivocal: No, she should not. How dare she even contemplate abandoning her saintly and heroic life for the mundane pleasures of marriage? The very thought appalled him. In her next letter, Isotta conceded that he might have a point. The celibate path she had chosen, though hard, was far nobler. Indeed, such were its virtues that she now urged her dear friend Foscarini to forsake his own worldly existence and follow her example. They could be pious recluses together.

Foscarini fired back a swift refusal. How could she imagine such a possibility for a servant of the Venetian empire, a husband and father, a man with all his pressing domestic obligations and civic responsibilities? He, unlike Isotta, had no need to suppress his emotional needs in order to enjoy the life of the mind. Isotta might belong to the officially designated weaker sex, but she was the one who had to make hard choices. So the unnamed suitor was duly sent away disappointed, and—until her death at the age of 48—Isotta remained alone.

Antonello da Messina's *Virgin Annunciate* of 1474 portrays the Madonna not in heavenly glory but in earthly humility, eschewing the opulence of medieval art for more modest dress and a book of prayer. Images and icons like this were common in Renaissance homes, aiding children and adults in their religious devotions.

Women, for example, would contemplate pictures of female saints and emulate their virtues. "Truly, the virginity of Mary is put forth to you as the exemplar of all sanctity," the Veronese canon Paolo Maffei told Isotta Nogarola. "Never lose sight of her humility, her love, her modesty."

ORNAMENTS AND APPAREL

"Everyone should dress well, according to his age and his position in society," wrote Giovanni della Casa in his 16th-century etiquette book. "If he does not, it will be taken as a mark of contempt for other people." During the Renaissance, well-to-do Italians embraced this ideal, employing tailors and embroiderers to create exquisite clothing, such as that worn by guests at the Florentine wedding shown at right.

The quality of the fabrics—fine linens and wools, silks, damasks, and the new brocaded velvets—was unsurpassed. Silver and gold threads woven into cloth and the addition of pearls and other jewels enhanced its beauty—and raised its price. The wealthy indulged themselves, however: Lorenzo de' Medici, known as Lorenzo the Magnificent, owned 30 or more robes—several of which cost more than a middle-class family of four might spend in one year.

The money lavished on such finery moved local governments to pass sumptuary laws. In 1452, for example, some women who attended a wedding in Bologna wearing prohibited brocades and colors were excommunicated. Many women vigorously opposed the restrictions, saying their appearance proclaimed their standing in society. "Ornaments and apparel," wrote a noblewoman in 1453, "are our insignia of worth."

Two Venetian ladies relax with their pets in this painting from about 1500. Their low-cut necklines bordered with pearls represent the more daring styles popular in the northern cities of Venice and Milan. More conventional are their detachable sleeves, which are slit to allow the sleeves of the underdresses to show through. Narrow ties affix each sleeve to the gown's shoulder and join the sleeves at intervals along their length.

Platform shoes *(left)* kept the hem of the wearer's dress from dragging in the mud. Teetering on soles that ranged from four to 12 inches high, fashionable ladies were supported by their maids as they walked.

LADIES' FASHIONS: LAYERS OF FINERY

For warmth as well as fashion, women typically dressed in three layers: a linen chemise, an underdress of wool or silk, and an ornate overdress. Overdresses, usually sewn from the finest fabrics, could be understated—a style preferred by older women—or embellished with intricate embroidery, precious stones, or fur linings.

Dress designs ranged from gowns that hung straight from the shoulders, to high-waisted styles that gathered just under the bust, to those having a natural waist. Trains were a fashionable feature, but usually skirts just skimmed the floor. Voluminous sleeves were in vogue early in the 15th century, but over the years tighter sleeves became popular, with openings in the seams to allow underlying fabrics to show through.

The Florentine women facing each other wear gold-brocade gowns with their family insignia of doves and sunbursts woven into the fabric. Open at the sides, the gown at right reveals a patterned underdress. The gown of the woman at far left also allows a glimpse of her underdress, its V neck framing a laced bodice as well as the chemise beneath it.

With her hairline tweezed to create an artificially high forehead—and the illusion of height—this woman tucks her blond hair under a cap embroidered with pearls and gold thread. A transparent veil edged with gold and pearls completes the headdress. Short, triangular veils were preferred by young women; older women chose shoulder-length rectangular veils.

While using the protective brim of a hat to shield her skin, a woman exposes her hair to the bleaching rays of the sun. Blond hair was desirable among women; men were known to dye their hair black.

FINISHING TOUCHES: HEADDRESSES AND JEWELRY

To complete their ensembles, Renaissance women typically coiffured their hair carefully and topped it with an elaborate headdress. In some cases, the hair itself was removed: According to author Giovanni Boccaccio, hairdressers would "flay their ladies, plucking their brows and foreheads" to give them the appearance of greater height. When more-natural styles came into fashion, women took to braiding or coiling their hair on top of their heads.

Jewelry was an important accessory, especially as necklines plunged late in the 1400s. And although sumptuary laws attempted to limit the display of expensive jewelry—even restricting the number of rings one could wear—fashion-conscious women found ways to skirt the laws.

In lieu of headdresses, some women wrapped their hair tightly around their heads, weaving thin veils into the coils, in the style of the two women shown below.

In addition to her necklace of large gems and pearls, this young woman *(right)* wears a matching jeweled headband. Brooches, hatpins, and gems were often attached to headwear.

A young Venetian wears a knee-length tunic with wide sleeves and laces at the neck, which expose the shirt worn underneath *(far left).* The young man beside him—a nobleman holding a falcon—wears a richly detailed doublet with open sleeves.

In this artist's study, a young man's shirttail hangs below his doublet. His hip-high hose are laced to eyelets along the doublet's bottom edge.

THE BASICS OF A MAN'S WARDROBE

Renaissance men's attire consisted of three basic components: a long-sleeved shirt of fine linen; a doublet, or close-fitting jacket; and hose that were woven or stitched from cloth. Doublets usually had low collars and long sleeves, and they frequently ended just below the waist—although the length varied somewhat with fashion. The hose, which had soles of leather so that shoes were not necessary, were fastened to the lower edge of the doublet with ties.

Older men, especially officials and academics, sometimes wore long, stately robes over their other clothing, and young men donned knee-length tunics. During the first part of the 15th century, these tunics were pleated and cinched at the waist with belts; their very full sleeves became the target of sumptuary laws.

In his two-tone stockings and voluminous tunic, the very stylish Sienese gentleman at left contrasts sharply with the soberly dressed Florentines at right. Their plain but richly colored robes have detachable rolled-brim hoods.

CHAPTER TWO

BONFIRES OF THE VANITIES

Lorenzo de' Medici wears the plain costume of the common citizen in this bust by Andrea del Verrocchio, but the set of his jaw and furrowed brow hint at his onerous role as leader of the Florentine republic. A prince in every respect but title, Lorenzo labored to preserve peace with other city-states while securing his position against hostile fellow patricians.

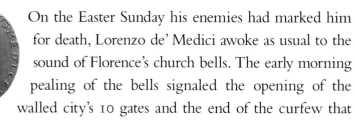

On the Easter Sunday his enemies had marked him for death, Lorenzo de' Medici awoke as usual to the sound of Florence's church bells. The early morning pealing of the bells signaled the opening of the walled city's 10 gates and the end of the curfew that kept practically everyone off the streets from sunset to sunrise. Through the few windows of his fortresslike palace, Lorenzo could hear the narrow, winding streets begin to come to life.

As he arose that morning in April 1478, Lorenzo thought of the distinguished young guest he would later escort to High Mass at the cathedral: Cardinal Raffaele Riario, the 17-year-old grandnephew of Pope Sixtus IV. Lorenzo often hosted visiting dignitaries, but Riario was special. For several years now Lorenzo had been feuding with the pope, and he hoped a show of hospitality to Riario would improve relations. After the cardinal celebrated Mass, Lorenzo would show him the treasures of his home—the paintings, sculptures, and antiquities that made the Palazzo Medici one of the showcases of the city. And later that day he would give a great banquet in the young cleric's honor.

Hosting the rich and powerful was just one of Lorenzo's functions as Florence's leading citizen. Though nominally a republic, this thriving city-state, with its surrounding Tuscan countryside and communities, was controlled by a small number of patrician families. Foremost among them was the powerful banking family, the Medici. As head of the Medici family, Lorenzo was the acknowledged political leader of Florence.

Lorenzo did not quite look—or sound—the part. Tall and robust, he resembled an athlete more than a statesman. He liked plain, dark-colored clothing. His face was swarthy with a stern brow and a heavy jaw that jutted so far forward his lower lip nearly enclosed the upper; his large, flat nose, which lacked all sense of smell, looked broken. His voice was nasal and high pitched.

But what made this Medici so attractive to most of Florence was his infectious zest for living. Lorenzo seemed interested in virtually everything—and good at most of it. He studied Plato, played the lyre, and made architectural drawings. At his country villas, he gardened, raised pigs and pheasants, bred racehorses, hunted and fished, experimented with cheesemaking, and talked endlessly with the artists, writers, and scholars he invited there to discuss classical texts and philosophical mysteries. He composed poetry in the Tuscan dialect. He wrote devout hymns and bawdy songs. He sponsored public masquerades and pageants, engaging the finest artists to design masks and decorate the floats and writing lively songs that celebrated the moment: "Seize on pleasure, those who wish to; / For tomorrow's not a certainty."

Lorenzo's intellect and energy were matched by his competitive drive. "He did not want to be equaled or imitated even in verses or games or exercises and turned angrily on anyone who did so," wrote one contemporary. Not yet 30 years old, he was already a prototype for what was later called the Renaissance man.

Before Mass, Lorenzo would have had breakfast with his wife, Clarice, and their three young children in the family's apartment above the palace's ground floor. He probably discussed with his wife last-minute details of the banquet for Cardinal Riario.

Clarice was a Roman by birth and eager to help her husband mend fences with the pope. Her family was one of the most powerful in Rome, and Lorenzo had married her at his family's behest for political reasons. The couple shared affection, if not love, but few interests beyond the children. And as was the custom among Florentine males of his class, Lorenzo took mistresses, as his schedule permitted.

That morning he may also have looked in on his brother, Giuliano, who lived in a separate apartment in the palace and who would later join Lorenzo and his guest at the cathedral. Four years younger than Lorenzo, Giuliano loved music and poetry and the public jousting tournaments that the Medici sponsored. But he had no interest in politics, and he was happy to leave the cares of government and business to his brother.

In yet another of the palace's apartments, set aside for his use, Cardinal Riario was changing into his vestments. Shortly after 11:00 a.m., Lorenzo went downstairs to meet him. Then the two walked through a statue-lined inner courtyard and out onto the Via Larga through the immense iron gates of the Palazzo Medici.

The Palazzo Medici was the house built three decades earlier by Lorenzo's grandfather, Cosimo de' Medici. Cosimo had made certain its ground floor was large enough to contain offices and counting houses for the family's business enterprises, as well as a lavish banquet hall and a private chapel with marble floor and magnificent frescoes painted by Benozzo Gozzoli. During Cosimo's lifetime, the household had once consisted of no fewer than 50 persons. A visitor, marveling at all the storerooms, kitchens and pantries, wells, latrines, and servants' quarters, commented that Cosimo "has not left out anything that is convenient."

Cosimo had not only built this splendid structure but helped create the commercial and political edifice known as the House of Medici as well. He had inherited from his father in 1428 what was already the largest banking firm in Europe, with branches in 16 capitals. Cosimo then shrewdly expanded the bank into an

Like many buildings of Renaissance Florence, the Palazzo Medici has the appearance of a stronghold. Filippo Brunelleschi had designed a grander palace for Cosimo de' Medici, Lorenzo's grandfather, but the prudent banker, envisioning the envy it would elicit, chose this more austere design by Michelozzo Michelozzi. Even so, when it was completed in the 1450s, one rival accused Cosimo of commissioning "a palace that throws even the Colosseum at Rome into the shade."

Displayed on the corner of the building is a Medici coat of arms similar to the one above, with red balls, or *palle*, on a gold field. The balls may represent pills, giving rise to speculation that the Medici—as their name implies—at one time were associated with the practice of medicine.

Dominating this 15th-century view of Florence are the cathedral and the Palazzo della Signoria, seats of spiritual and political power, and the Arno River, which contributed greatly to the city-state's economic strength. Although it could generate devastating floods, the Arno was the city's lifeblood, providing textile workers with water to process cloth, flour mills with power to grind grain, and traders with access to the sea 50 miles away. The river also provided fish and wildfowl for the city's food supply, running water for sanitation, and—not least—beauty for the aesthetic appetites of Florentines.

even more prosperous business empire, embracing the manufacture of silk and woolen goods, the trading of spices and other prized products from the Far East, and the marketing of alum, a transparent mineral salt essential in making dyes and glass. One of the richest men in Florence, he became a generous patron of churches and the humanities, financing the reconstruction of San Lorenzo and San Marco, and collecting and preserving ancient books and manuscripts from all over Europe.

In the political realm, Cosimo also eventually reigned supreme—but only after he had learned a priceless lesson in power. Florence in those days was governed by a nine-man municipal council known as the Signoria. Eight members were selected by lot. Their names were drawn from eight leather bags containing the names of men deemed eligible for office because of membership in the 21 guilds that represented Florence's merchants, professionals, and artisans. The eight members then chose a ninth, the gonfalonier of justice, who acted as chairman. During their two-month terms the members met twice a day in the Palazzo della Signoria, the Signoria palace.

Florentines took pride in this process. But it was scarcely democratic. To begin with, it excluded most citizens: About 80 percent of the city's men worked outside the privileges and protection of the guilds, and in all, only 6,000 male guild members aged 30 and over could be considered for office. Moreover, the system was dominated by Florence's richest families, who often became bitter rivals for power. The Albizzi, for example, hated the Medici. They were jealous of Cosimo's well-publicized good works—it was said "even the monks' privies" were inscribed with the Medici family crest—and were still fuming over an old tax reform supported by Cosimo's father that was perceived to have favored the poor. In 1433 the Albizzi won a majority in the Signoria and had Cosimo exiled to Padua.

Scarcely a year later, a friendly new Signoria allowed him to return to Florence. As a result of his experiences, Cosimo was determined to take control of the city government. This he achieved not so much by holding public office, though he did for a brief time serve as gonfalonier. Rather, he preferred to operate behind the scenes, creating a political machine through the judicious use of gifts and loans. Soon he was recognized, at home and abroad, as the de facto head of the republic. At his death in 1464, that position passed to his son Piero and, after Piero's death five years later, to Piero's son Lorenzo.

Only 20 years old at the time, Lorenzo had already been sent on diplomatic missions by his father and had absorbed the lessons of power at his grandfather's knee. It was not long before he, too, was caught up in a classic power struggle of the kind that nearly destroyed Cosimo. His rivals were the Pazzi, an old-line family of nobles. The Pazzi had become the second leading family of bankers in Florence, but the Medici had denied them the public offices and honors to which they felt entitled. The simmering intrigues of the rivalry were complicated by the involvement of a third party, none other than the pope himself, Sixtus IV.

Sixtus and the Medici had initially enjoyed cordial relations. Lorenzo had headed the Florentine delegation at his coronation in 1471, and the Medici bank had acquired the lucrative job of managing the papal finances. Relations quickly soured, however. Popes at this time were infamous for their self-interest and greed, but Sixtus demonstrated an unprecedented bent for nepotism. He made cardinals out of six of his nephews and displayed a ruthless determination to strengthen his political power in the Papal States and beyond. He and Lorenzo first clashed over the matter of Imola, which stood strategically between Florence and the Adriatic. Sixtus had learned that Lorenzo was trying to purchase the town for Florence and decided to buy it himself. When the Medici bank refused to lend the pope funds for the transaction, he turned to the rival Pazzi family. The Pazzi promptly made the loan and proceeded to take over the pope's finances from the Medici bank.

Other issues fed the papal feud. Sixtus appointed as arch-

As many as 30,000 people could crowd into Florence's cathedral to hear sermons by one of the many charismatic preachers of the day. Begun in 1296, the cathedral was not completed until 1436, when Brunelleschi finished the construction of its huge dome, the largest since Roman times. Beyond being a place of worship, the cathedral was a monument of civic pride.

bishop of Pisa a member of another Florentine family hostile to the Medici, the Salviati. The Tuscan port city of Pisa was controlled by Florence, and Lorenzo retaliated by refusing to allow archbishop-designate Francesco Salviati to assume his post. Lorenzo then irritated Sixtus further by arranging a triple alliance with Venice and Milan that confronted the Papal States with strong and united northern neighbors.

Sixtus grew so enraged with the Medici that he agreed to support a conspiracy to oust them from power. The prime conspirators were Archbishop Salviati and Francesco

In this portrait by Sandro Botticelli, the downcast eyes of Giuliano de' Medici signify his premature death, the dove symbolizes mourning for him, and the open window is a sign of his passage to the afterlife.

de' Pazzi, manager of the family bank in Rome. The pope's instructions were specific. "I do not want anyone killed, just a change in the government," he told them. "Go, and do what you wish, provided there be no killing."

Killing, however, was precisely what the conspirators had in mind. They intended to assassinate both Lorenzo and his younger brother, Giuliano, then seize power in the ensuing confusion. The attack would take place in the cathedral during the celebration of High Mass on Easter Sunday, 1478, when Cardinal Riario—who was not privy to the plot—was to be the Medici guest of honor.

Florence's magnificent cathedral lay only a short walk away from the Palazzo Medici, and that Easter morning Lorenzo and young Riario decided to walk. Along the Via Larga they were met by Francesco Salviati, the archbishop whom Lorenzo had kept from taking his post in Pisa. Chatting amiably, Salviati walked with them part of the way. Before reaching the cathedral he excused himself. His mother was seriously ill, Salviati told them, and he was on his way to visit her. He was, in fact, headed for the Palazzo della Signoria, some 400 yards to the south, by the Arno River, to play his assigned role in the plot: seizing the seat of government.

Upon entering the cathedral, Lorenzo took Riario to the high altar and then walked over to chat with a group of friends gathered on the right side of the nave. Since churches of the day did not have pews, congregants could move about freely before Mass, and this time often became an occasion for gossip, political conversation, and even the settling of business transactions.

While Lorenzo socialized, his brother, Giuliano, arrived at the now crowded cathedral and found himself a place on the left side of the nave. Nearby hovered his appointed assassins, Francesco de' Pazzi and Bernardo di Bandini Baroncelli, a former Pazzi business associate.

The service began, and eventually Cardinal Riario un-

knowingly gave the signal the conspirators had been waiting for: He lifted the Host, the consecrated bread of Holy Communion, and the congregants bowed their heads. At that moment the assassins struck. From behind Giuliano's lowered head came the cry, "Take that, traitor!" and Baroncelli brought his dagger down with such force that it nearly split his victim's skull in two. Then Francesco fell upon Giuliano, stabbing him no fewer than 18 times and accidentally slashing his own leg in his fury.

At the same moment Giuliano fell, his brother was being attacked on the other side of the cathedral. Lorenzo's intended assassins, a pair of priests that hated the Medici, had taken up position behind him. At the agreed-upon signal one of them—inexpertly—placed his hand on Lorenzo's shoulder to steady himself as he thrust the dagger. Lorenzo turned, felt the point cut into his neck, and leaped away. Drawing his sword, he slashed at his surprised assailants. Then he vaulted over the altar rail and dashed past a horrified Cardinal Riario toward the sacristy.

In pursuit, racing through the bewildered congregants, came Giuliano's assassin, Francesco. He struck down and killed one of Lorenzo's friends and wounded another. But before he could reach the sacristy, Lorenzo and several of his companions were safely through its heavy bronze doors, which they barred behind them. Inside the sacristy, among the stored vestments and sacred vessels, a friend sucked blood from the wound on Lorenzo's neck in case the priest's dagger had been tipped with poison. Lorenzo kept asking about Giuliano. No one had the heart to tell him: His brother was dead.

At the Palazzo della Signoria, meanwhile, Archbishop Salviati had arrived with a band of armed mercenaries disguised as attendants. Claiming that he carried an urgent message from the pope, he was admitted to the official chambers upstairs. But once inside the building he managed to get separated from his supporters. Moreover, he appeared extremely agitated, and the city officials began to suspect some treachery. Taking no chances, the gonfalonier called out the palace guard and had Salviati arrested. When word of Giuliano's murder reached the palace, a rope was tied around the archbishop's neck, and he was hanged from one of the building's upper-story windows.

The people of Florence eventually put to death some 80 others either connected with the conspiracy or suspected of sympathizing with it. Among them was Francesco de' Pazzi. Still bleeding from the self-inflicted wound in his thigh, Giuliano's assassin was found hiding at home and dragged to the Palazzo della Signoria. To the cheers of the

The 1479 execution of anti-Medici conspirator Bernardo di Bandini Baroncelli was sketched by Leonardo da Vinci, who noted in his customary backward script what the hanged man was wearing. Although Baroncelli had escaped to Constantinople after murdering Giuliano, Lorenzo de' Medici persuaded the sultan to extradite him to Florence.

crowd congregating in the piazza below, Francesco was hanged alongside the dangling body of Salviati.

Pope Sixtus—"the fountain-head and instigator of all ill," as Lorenzo now called him—was infuriated at the failure of the anti-Medici plot. In response to the execution of the archbishop-designate of Pisa, he seized the Medici bank assets in Rome, suspended all religious services in Florence, and excommunicated Lorenzo and other prominent citizens. Lorenzo was unrepentant. "I have committed no crime against the Pope, save that I am alive," he wrote the king of France. "This is my sin."

At length, Sixtus declared war on Florence and persuaded his powerful neighbor to the south, King Ferdinand I of Naples, to join in. Their forces invaded Tuscany and quickly defeated the Florentine army, which consisted solely of mercenaries. By December 1479 Lorenzo saw that his city's plight was desperate. Convinced that the war was directed at him personally, he decided upon a bold move. Secretly he left Florence, made his way to Pisa, and boarded a ship bound for Naples. Behind him he left a letter to the Signoria explaining his actions. "By delivering myself into their hands," wrote Lorenzo, he might "be the means of restoring peace to our fellow-citizens."

Although the risks of such an undertaking were considerable, Lorenzo had

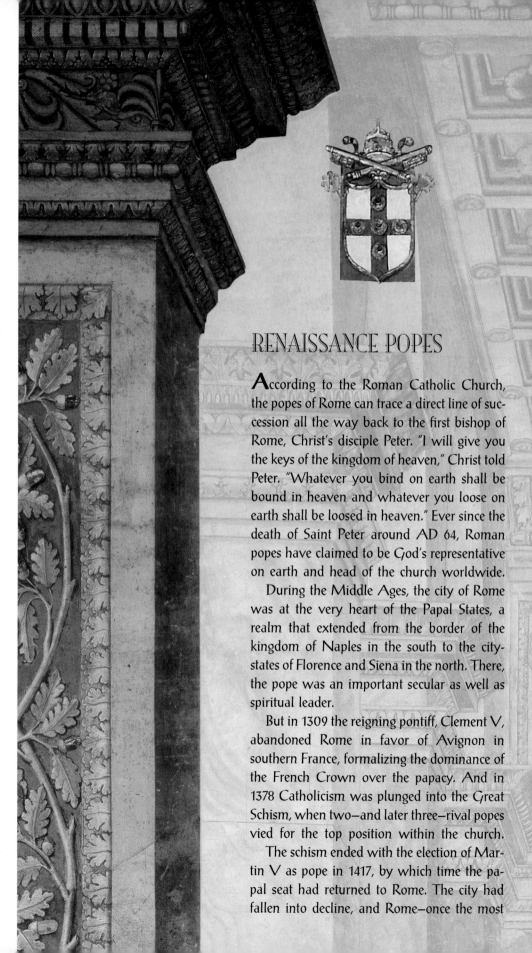

RENAISSANCE POPES

According to the Roman Catholic Church, the popes of Rome can trace a direct line of succession all the way back to the first bishop of Rome, Christ's disciple Peter. "I will give you the keys of the kingdom of heaven," Christ told Peter. "Whatever you bind on earth shall be bound in heaven and whatever you loose on earth shall be loosed in heaven." Ever since the death of Saint Peter around AD 64, Roman popes have claimed to be God's representative on earth and head of the church worldwide.

During the Middle Ages, the city of Rome was at the very heart of the Papal States, a realm that extended from the border of the kingdom of Naples in the south to the city-states of Florence and Siena in the north. There, the pope was an important secular as well as spiritual leader.

But in 1309 the reigning pontiff, Clement V, abandoned Rome in favor of Avignon in southern France, formalizing the dominance of the French Crown over the papacy. And in 1378 Catholicism was plunged into the Great Schism, when two—and later three—rival popes vied for the top position within the church.

The schism ended with the election of Martin V as pope in 1417, by which time the papal seat had returned to Rome. The city had fallen into decline, and Rome—once the most

A 15th-century fresco of the walled city of Rome depicts some of the ancient structures so greatly admired by the humanists: the Colosseum *(center, left)*, the Pantheon *(center, right)*, and the Arch of Septimius Severus *(in front of Colosseum)*. The city was transformed into a new Renaissance capital by the popes who lived there.

Shown here at his 1458 coronation, Pius II was an accomplished author, scholar, and humanist. His official ring *(above)* bore his seal on top; as custom required, upon Pius's death in 1464 the seal was broken and replaced with a gemstone.

Raphael may have painted this portrait of Julius II—who was 60 years old when elected pope—from a death mask. Julius left a legacy of papal artistic patronage, including Michelangelo's Sistine Chapel ceiling, Bramante's St. Peter's, and Raphael's Vatican frescoes in the papal apartments.

Sixtus IV appoints the humanist Platina as head of the Vatican library. Sixtus is best known for his blatant nepotism; beside Platina stands the pope's nephew, Cardinal Giuliano della Rovere, the future Pope Julius II.

Although his appeal is by no means evident in this portrait, Alexander VI—Rodrigo Borgia—was a notorious womanizer who fathered numerous children, including Lucrezia and Cesare. He was also a generous patron of the arts, lending his support to Raphael, Michelangelo, Bramante, and other outstanding talents of the day.

Julius's successor, the extravagant and cultured Leo X (above), was the second son of Lorenzo de' Medici and the pope responsible for excommunicating the Protestant reformer Martin Luther.

magnificent capital of the Western world—had become a dilapidated provincial town full of ruins. But these were the very ruins that Renaissance humanists were beginning to revere, the remnants of a once great classical civilization: Rome was about to undergo its own Renaissance.

Over the course of the 15th century a series of popes launched a rebuilding program that returned the city to its former grandeur. Extravagant, worldly, and often immoral, these Renaissance popes were as much concerned with the temporal power of their office as they were with the ecclesiastical functions of the church, as much devoted to the arts as they were to God.

Among them were Pius II (1458-1464), whose papacy was marked by artistic patronage and the encouragement of humanist education; Sixtus IV (1471-1484), a learned Franciscan who bribed his way into office, established the Spanish Inquisition, and built the Sistine Chapel; Alexander VI (1492-1503), perhaps the most infamous of all, who lived openly with his mistress in the Vatican and secured prominent positions for many of his kin; Julius II (1503-1513), an excellent administrator, military strategist, and diplomat who began the rebuilding of St. Peter's basilica in Rome and commissioned Michelangelo to paint the Sistine ceiling; and Leo X (1513-1521), during whose time papal power and extravagance reached its peak.

These leaders of the church established artistic legacies, if not moral ones, and revitalized Rome. But their worldliness and corruption were also responsible for the upheavals that swept Christendom in the 16th century. Leo's continuation of Julius II's practice of selling indulgences in order to finance the building of a new St. Peter's prompted Martin Luther's protest in Wittenberg, an act that eventually brought about the Reformation.

worked shrewdly to reduce them. He already had communicated with the court in Naples to make certain he would not be treated harshly. And as insurance, he took with him bagfuls of gold florins, raised by mortgaging one of his country estates, so that he could dispense goodwill to charities and other deserving hands.

In Naples, Lorenzo was both prisoner and guest. He wooed King Ferdinand with wit and charm, and the two men hunted together and talked poetry. Lorenzo also discussed military and political matters and emphasized to the king the dangers to Naples if Florence were dismembered and the pope became too powerful. Finally, in March 1480, after 10 weeks in Naples, Lorenzo returned to Florence—and a tumultuous welcome. In his pocket he carried a peace treaty with the Neapolitan king.

Lorenzo's gift for diplomacy helped keep the peace in the Italian peninsula for the next dozen years. He united Florence with Naples against Pope Sixtus. Then, when Venice threatened the balance of power, he formed an alliance with the successor pope, Innocent VIII, cementing relations by marrying off one of his daughters to a son Innocent had fathered before becoming a priest. And in what he termed "the greatest achievement of our house," he persuaded the pope—almost certainly with the customary bribes—to

Jugs of medicinal herbs and spices line the shelves of this apothecary shop, which also sold sweets, candles, stationery, jewelry, and artists' supplies. By the late 15th century, more than five dozen druggists served Florence's population. Their shops were strictly regulated by the doctors and apothecaries guild, which monitored prices and the accuracy of scales, such as the set shown on the counter.

promise to make a cardinal of his son Giovanni, who was then only 13 years old. Giovanni one day would himself be elected to the papacy as Leo X.

Lorenzo's successes abroad as well as his generosity at home won for him the title Il Magnifico. He presided over what would become known as a golden age of culture. He created a training center for young artists and took into the Palazzo Medici a 15-year-old painter named Michelangelo Buonarroti, who was given his own room and a place at the family table. At the same time, however, fewer florins flowed into good works from the House of Medici. For although Lorenzo shared his grandfather's open-handed instincts, he lacked Cosimo's taste and talent for business, and under Il Magnifico the Medici bank fell into decline.

Trouble loomed on the political front, too. Voices of dissent were raised against Lorenzo, and he was increasingly labeled a tyrant. His loudest critic was a young priest named Girolamo Savonarola, who hurled verbal thunderbolts at Lorenzo from the pulpit of San Marco, the church most heavily endowed by the Medici. When a group of prominent citizens tried to persuade the upstart cleric to temper his criticism, Savonarola was blunt. "Go and tell Lorenzo to repent of his sins," he told them, "for God will punish him and his."

But while Savonarola's sermons drew large crowds, the majority of Florentines would probably have agreed with a contemporary historian about Lorenzo: "If Florence was to have a tyrant, she could never have found a better or more delightful one." Even so, Lorenzo did seem to take Savonarola's criticisms to heart. In spring of 1492, suffering from gout and a severe stomach disorder compounded by a concoction of pulverized pearls and precious stones prescribed by his physicians, Lorenzo called for the priest. Savonarola came to his bedside and gave him absolution. A few days later, on April 8, Lorenzo died at the age of 43. He was buried across the street from the Palazzo Medici in the sacristy of San Lorenzo, next to his brother, Giuliano—the one who had not escaped the murder in the cathedral 14 years before.

Situated on the busy Via Tornabuoni, Luca Landucci's apothecary shop buzzed with excitement and anxiety. Between dispensing herbs and medical advice—his cure for a nosebleed was to hold the nose with two fingers while reciting prayers—Luca traded the latest political news with his customers. And today all the gossip was about the foreign army poised to enter Florence.

Had not Savonarola predicted it? Luca might well have asked his patrons. "The sword of God is about to strike the earth," the priest had prophesied repeatedly, and it would smite the sinful Florentines in the form of foreign enemies pouring across the Alps like "barbers armed with gigantic razors." Now it was hap-

pening. Only a week before—two years after the death of Lorenzo—the Medici had been ousted from power because of the coming of these enemies. A huge French army had invaded northern Italy, and the king of France himself, Charles VIII, was about to ride in triumph through the streets of Florence.

Luca had seen many things over the years. A mild-mannered, kindhearted man of 58, he had been in the apothecary trade since his teens, when he began an apprenticeship in a shop in the bustling Old Market, the Mercato Vecchio. Along with doctors, apothecaries stood high in the city's guild structure, and were deemed part of the *popolo grasso*—"the well-fed people."

Luca was fortunate, too, in his marriage. His wife, Salvestra, he wrote, was "a dear companion, and unequalled for virtue," who never once gave him "cause for anger." She did give him a dozen children and a dowry of 400 florins. The dowry had enabled him to set up shop in one of the busiest sections of the city. The only problem with the location was the dust and congestion caused by the construction of the Palazzo Strozzi on the other side of the street, which had started five years previously and seemed never to end.

But what would single out Luca Landucci in the eyes of history was the diary he kept. For 66 years, from 1450 until his death in 1516, he jotted down the news of Florence as he witnessed it or heard it from customers and well-placed sources in the government. He wrote about the weather and about the periodic flooding of the Arno. He noted the state of the grapes, the figs, and the corn. And he recorded the religious and political events of the city. Recently the political news had been dominated by the coming of the French and the fate of the House of Medici.

Upon Lorenzo's death in 1492, Piero de' Medici had inherited his father's position as head of the Florentine republic. But what Piero had *not* inherited was Lorenzo's delicate touch in dealing with domestic allies and potential foreign foes. These shortcomings had been all too apparent when Charles VIII crossed the Alps into Italy in the fall of 1494 to press France's old claim to the kingdom of Naples.

Charles had demanded safe passage for his army through Tuscany, and the 22-year-old Piero had vacillated. First, he supported Naples. Then, with the French advancing on him, Piero impulsively tried to emulate his father's bold stroke of 15 years earlier during the war with the pope and Naples by going directly into the enemy camp.

When Piero met Charles at his camp near the Tuscan border, however, he caved in to all the king's demands. He surrendered Pisa—which Charles promptly freed from Florentine rule—as well as several western Florentine fortresses that would protect the rear of the French army as it moved south. He even granted Charles a generous loan of 200,000 florins to finance his military campaign. Members of the Signoria, who had not been consulted by Piero, were outraged when they learned of these concessions, and they forced Piero and his entire family into exile. For the first time in 60 years, no Medici dominated Florence. With a mixture of hope and trepidation the people of the city anticipated the coming of the French.

Like everyone else in Florence, Luca Landucci was eager to see the arrival of King Charles. On the afternoon of Monday, November 17, 1494, he closed his shop early and hurried to the cathedral, the king's first stop within the city walls. Along the way Luca noticed signs of the coming military occupation—the chalk marks on doors that identified which houses would become billets for French soldiers.

The king's entry was, indeed, grand. He wore gilt armor, a crown, and a cloak of gold cloth, and sat astride a great black warhorse, his lance upraised in the traditional manner of the conqueror. Flanked by his generals, he rode through the streets under a canopy held above his head by four mounted knights. Behind him came the royal bodyguard, as well as some 19,000 splendidly attired troops: 10,000 infantrymen, 3,000 cavalry, 4,000 archers, and 2,000 crossbowmen.

The procession moved slowly through the narrow, crowded streets, and the sun had already set by the time the king reached the cathedral. But none of the citizens had gone home. "All Florence was there," Luca observed, "either in the church or outside." And they had been instructed by the Signoria to give the French a rapturous welcome. "Everyone shouted," recalled Luca, "great and small, old and young."

Luca noted a change come over the crowd when the king dismounted to enter the cathedral. "When he was seen on foot he seemed to the people somewhat less imposing, for he was in fact a very small man." Moreover, as he made his way up the torch-

Charles VIII and his troops parade past the Palazzo Medici *(at left)* in this painting by Francesco Granacci, which records the entry of the French army into the city-state of Florence on November 17, 1494. Although the French eventually left peacefully, Florence never recovered its sense of inviolability.

These terra-cotta emblems by Luca Della Robbia and his nephew Andrea represent two of the Florentine guilds: physicians and apothecaries *(top)* and masons and carpenters *(bottom)*. The guilds were active in all aspects of city life, from determining the annual number of working days to ensuring that the merchant class had a political voice.

lit nave to the cathedral's high altar, he leaned forward, limping slightly on what appeared to be outsize feet. The rumor quickly spread that the diminutive Frenchman had six toes on each foot.

The cheers of the Florentines soon returned, however. After Mass, Charles remounted his horse and—to cries of *"Viva Francia!"*—made his way to the Palazzo Medici, where he would reside during his stay in the city.

The French king soon dashed Luca's expressed "hopes that he would bring us peace and rest." Because Piero de' Medici had proved so accommodating, Charles demanded his restoration to power. The Signoria refused, threatening to take up arms to resist. As tensions mounted, some citizens began to throw stones at the foreign soldiers. Fearing the worst, Luca and other shopkeepers closed their premises and stayed home. "Fear was so widespread," wrote Luca, "the whole of Florence locked itself in."

In desperation, the prophetic priest Girolamo Savonarola was sent to plead with the king on behalf of the city. But Savonarola did much more: He hailed Charles as the liberator of Florence, a minister of justice, an instrument of God. But God, he said, wanted Charles to be kind to Florence, and the French delay in leaving the city was displeasing to him.

Eventually, Savonarola's words—plus the Signoria's agreement to pay the French a handsome ransom—had their intended effect. The king and his army left Florence and headed south to capture Naples. In the eyes of Luca Landucci and many of his fellow citizens, Savonarola had worked a miracle. The 42-year-old friar was hailed as the city's special prophet.

Savonarola's rise to prominence was all the more remarkable in that he was a foreigner, not a Florentine. A native of Ferrara, he was the son and grandson of physicians. His grandfather, doctor to Duke Alfonso d'Este, was an exponent of the beneficial effects of spa waters and alcohol. But young Girolamo had been more interested in the anatomy of the soul. He wrote poetry, played the lute, and, after a traumatic rejection by his chosen loved one, left home to enter a Dominican monastery in Bologna. He was nearly 23 years old and, he wrote his father, "unable any longer to endure the evil doing of the heedless people of Italy."

Savonarola was an unattractive man—small and thin with a huge, hooked nose and thick fleshy lips and green eyes that flashed beneath heavy black eyebrows—and in the beginning not much of a preacher. But in Florence, where the Dominicans sent him in 1481, he found his voice. It was simple and unadorned, but powerfully apocalyptic. From the pulpit of San Marco he denounced other members of the clergy, the papacy, bankers, and tyrants as well as humanist literature and art. He attacked social injustice and the oppression of the poor, winning a reputation as the "preacher of the despairing." The people of Florence must repent, he declared, or doom awaited them.

Savonarola built up a substantial following, drawn by his passion and his sincerity; crowds often grew so large that he had to preach from the cathedral itself. Savonarola's own explanation of his impact was simple. "It is not I who preach," he declared, "but God who speaks through me."

Though some saw him as a traitor, Savonarola's authority increased in the wake of the French invasion. The crisis with the French had disrupted the economy, and the loss of Pisa had cost the city its lifeline to the sea; many shops remained closed, and much of the countryside lay fallow. The Florentines were desperate for guidance. Savonarola, having predicted some of the city's misfortunes, appeared to offer a chance for salvation through civic reform. According to Luca, he began preaching every day in the cathedral—frequently to crowds of up to 14,000—doing "his utmost in the pulpit to persuade Florence to adopt a good form of government." Savonarola announced that the city had been chosen by God as his center for the spiritual renewal of all Italy. "Florence," he promised, "will be more glorious, richer, more powerful than she has ever been."

Largely due to Savonarola's influence, the city adopted a new constitution that dramatically broadened representation in government after more than a half-century of Medici control. Taxes were reduced and a state loan office was set up to lend money to the poor at low rates of interest. The priest's intervention on the side of reform may have been decisive in averting civil strife. For Luca, though, Savonarola's grandest achievement was his impact on the youth, and in particular his transformation of the carnival that preceded Lent into a time of piety and good works.

Ordinarily during carnival the youths of the city engaged in stone throwing and other raucous behavior. But for the 1496 carnival, Savonarola gathered together some 6,000 boys between the ages of five and 16, ordered their hair cut short, and sent them into the streets in "bands of hope" to gather alms for the poor. On the final day of carnival, troops of the boys ceremonially assembled in the four quarters of the city. Carrying olive branches and singing praises to God, the boys converged on the cathedral, where they delivered the offering they had collected for the poor. Luca rejoiced with a father's pride: "Some of my sons were amongst those blessed and pure-minded troops of boys." Listening to all the boys singing in the cathedral, Luca thought that they

These Della Robbia plaques depict the symbols of the silk-manufacturers *(top)* and wool-workers *(bottom)* guilds. Along with the emblems opposite, they adorned the facade of Orsanmichele, a church that had been sponsored by Florence's artisans and tradesmen. The guilds commissioned numerous public works of art and architecture, including Michelangelo's *David.*

sounded like angels, and he "felt much spiritual comfort."

Savonarola also employed his young "bands of hope" as vice squads. Roaming the streets, they helped enforce new morality legislation the priest had pushed through, banning gambling, immodest dress, and profanity. Most people applauded the young crusaders. "If anyone had rebelled against them," observed Luca, "he would have been in danger of his life, whoever he was."

For the carnival of 1497 the friar had even greater things in mind for his children's crusade. That year both boys and girls were sent forth in search of what he called "vanities." Going from door to door all over the city, they collected anything considered vain or wicked: masks and costumes, mirrors, cosmetics, wigs, perfume, fancy dresses, musical instruments, and books and paintings that had been deemed lascivious or heretical. The children bore these in formal procession to the Piazza della Signoria. Everything, including precious manuscripts and works of art—some contributed in a burst of zeal by the authors and artists themselves—was heaped into a great pyramid 60 feet high. Then, to the ringing of bells, the blare of trumpets, and the chanting of a choir, white-robed children set ablaze Florence's first bonfire of vanities.

Inevitably, Savonarola's activities stirred

Colorful gondoliers crisscross the Grand Canal, and noblemen, merchants, pilgrims, and moneylenders crowd the walkways of the Rialto, the commercial hub of the Venetian republic.

A bird's-eye view of Venice shows the Grand Canal snaking its way through the city and the trading ships that linked Venetian merchants with the rest of the Mediterranean.

THE MOST SERENE REPUBLIC

Of all the city-states of Renaissance Italy, only one had an overseas empire: the republic of Venice. The empire consisted of the eastern coast of the Adriatic, the islands of Crete and Cyprus, and a large area of mainland Italy that was known as the Veneto. Its heart, however, was the archipelago on which the city of Venice itself was founded.

Venice had first been settled in 568, when hordes of Germanic Lombards descended on northern Italy and drove the natives of the region toward the Adriatic coast. There, on a collection of islands in a sheltered lagoon, developed a city-state that would one day become the most powerful trading empire of the Renaissance world.

During its early years Venice fell under the sway of Byzantium, whose capital in cosmopolitan Constantinople rivaled Rome as a center of Christendom. Venice, too, became a melting pot of cultures, a crossroads for east-west trade and travel. By the ninth century the city had developed into an independent republic, claiming Saint Mark the Evangelist as its patron saint and electing a doge—or duke—as its head of state.

In the centuries that followed, Venice gained control of trade throughout the Mediterranean region. In 1204 Venetian sailors and crusader knights sacked the city of Con-

Leonardo Loredan, doge from 1501-1521, wears the *cornu*, a horned hat that signified his position as head of the Venetian republic. Elected for life, doges led Venice for more than 1,000 years.

stantinople and carried much of its wealth back to Europe. In a war fought between 1378 and 1381, Venice defeated Genoa, its main maritime rival. During the 1400s Venice also expanded its mainland borders west to include Verona, Brescia, and Bergamo and east toward Trieste. And access to the rest of Europe was developed along a number of Alpine passes. Now Venice had a *stato da terra,* or land-state, as well as a *stato da mar,* or sea-state.

But it was the sea that provided Venice with the commerce that made this republic so successful: wine and sugar from the Aegean; silks, gems, perfumes, and dyes from Egypt and Asia Minor; gold, ivory, and slaves from Africa; tin from England;

wool and woven cloth from Flanders; and copper and steel from Germany. "Merchandise," declared one observer, "passes through this noble city as water flows through fountains."

The Venetians lavished much of their wealth on the beautification of their city, which by the 15th century rivaled Florence and Rome as a Renaissance capital of Italy. Tourists and pilgrims flocked there to view what one visiting German priest described as "the famous, great, wealthy, and noble city of Venice, the mistress of the Mediterranean, standing in wondrous fashion in the midst of the waters"—and what the Venetians themselves called La Serenissima Repubblica, the Most Serene Republic.

At the Venice shipyard known as the Arsenal *(top),* shipwrights build the trading vessels on which the republic's fortune was based. The biggest industrial complex in the Western world, the Arsenal had the ability to produce a new galley, like the one above, every 100 days.

The skill of Venetian glassblowers was renowned throughout the Renaissance world. The Murano glass goblet at right is named after the islands of Murano, where, for reasons of fire safety, all furnaces for glassblowing were confined.

divisive debate and even outright enmity. A powerful element of Florentines longed for the taverns, brothels, and gambling halls he had begun to close. Franciscans and other local clergy criticized him for his attacks on the church. Young aristocrats who opposed his advocacy of popular government sneered at his followers as *piagnoni*—"snivelers"—and they hired thugs to disrupt his sermons by banging on drums. But of all Savonarola's opponents, none was more dangerous than Pope Alexander VI.

Savonarola had earned Alexander's enmity not so much by his personal attacks on this pope, who was even more corrupt and unscrupulous than Sixtus IV—"a shameless harlot," according to the friar. What angered Alexander was Savonarola's friendship with the French. After King Charles conquered Naples, Alexander had formed a Holy League with Venice and Milan that eventually drove the French back across the Alps. It was a great Italian victory—but one in which Florence had played no part.

The city had remained neutral in the conflict at the bidding of Savonarola. In order to get Florence to join the Holy League, Alexander had tried to bribe him with a cardinal's red hat. The friar had been unmoved, proclaiming his preference for "one red with blood." Finally, in June 1497, the pope excommunicated him from the church.

As a result, many Florentines stopped attending Savonarola's sermons, the apothecary Luca Landucci among them; others voiced dismay that Florence had not helped in the expulsion of the French from Italy. Savonarola's support was beginning to ebb. Moreover, the city was now beset by other problems. Heavy rains ruined the crops in Tuscany, and Luca recorded grim reports of starvation: "Men, women, and children were falling down exhausted from hunger, and some died of it." There were also outbreaks of the plague and reports of a new disease called "French boils"—the syphilis spread by the recent invaders. Under increasing pressure from the pope, who ordered Florentine merchants living in Rome arrested and their goods seized, the Signoria tried to prevent Savonarola from preaching. But he continued. "I feel myself all burning, all inflamed with the spirit of the Lord," he told his congregation, and even wrote to the princes of Europe demanding that they call a council of reform to depose Pope Alexander.

In the spring of 1498 the tensions building in Florence sped to a climax. Skeptical of Savonarola's claims of divine inspiration, a Franciscan friar extended to Savonarola a challenge. He offered to undergo with Savonarola an ordeal by fire to prove that God had not granted the Dominican his special protection. Savonarola declined the challenge. Eventually surrogate priests—one a Dominican, the other a Franciscan—were selected by both men and the preparations made.

On April 7 the citizens of Florence flocked expectantly to the Piazza della Signoria. There in the middle of the piazza, just four feet apart, rose two great pyres of oil-soaked sticks; when the pyres were lighted, the two priests would have to walk a gauntlet 30 yards long between the fires. But the contestants wrangled all afternoon about what vestments could be worn and which religious objects carried, and much to the disappointment of the crowd, the scheduled ordeal fizzled out with the descent of night and a sudden downpour of rain.

The passions of the people had by now reached a fever pitch. Blood lust still blazed the next morning, Palm Sunday, when a mob attacked San Marco, Savonarola's monastery. At first the Dominicans defended themselves against the mob with clubs and swords. But Savonarola prevailed upon them to put down their weapons. As he calmly stood at the altar, ready for death, an armed guard arrived from the Signoria with orders for his arrest.

Despite his severe looks and apocalyptic sermons, Girolamo Savonarola attracted thousands of followers, including Fra Bartolommeo, who painted his portrait *(below).* Savonarola's attempts to establish a theocracy in Florence earned him powerful enemies, however, and in May 1498 the Dominican friar was sentenced to hang and burn. The execution in the *Piazza della Signoria* was mobbed, despite the sparsely attended depiction of it at left.

Girolamo Savonarola was taken to the Palazzo della Signoria, where a new government dominated by his enemies was now in power. In the palace's cells the friar was subjected to repeated torture on the rack. When the pain became unbearable for him, Savonarola confessed to anything his jailers demanded. But each time the torture ended, he would retract his confession. Three times this happened. Finally, with the bones of his left arm crushed and his will broken, he signed a written confession recanting his claim to divine inspiration. Together with two of his most fervent friar-disciples, he was found guilty of schism and heresy and sentenced to death.

On May 23, 1498, barefoot and unfrocked, the three priests were led to a scaffolding in the piazza. Thousands of Florentines came to witness the spectacle and enjoy the free food and drink supplied by the government. Savonarola kissed the crucifix he carried, and then he and his two companions were hanged from a gibbet and burned to ashes. Afterward, wrote Luca, carts "carried the last bit of dust to the Arno" to prevent the remains of the three men from being preserved and worshiped as holy relics.

Luca, like many of the prophet's followers, was profoundly shaken. He had heard the confession disavowing Savonarola's divine inspiration read aloud publicly, and when the condemned man failed to speak words of reassurance from his pyre, Luca felt sorely disappointed: "Everyone had been expecting some signs."

But the faithful kept watch for such a portent. Two weeks after the execution Luca reported the sudden emergence in the countryside of caterpillars that turned the color of gold after four days. The young boys who had carried out the friar's crusades called them "Fra Girolamo's caterpillars." The creatures appeared to have human faces with crowns on their heads and even halos and little crosses. As quickly as they had appeared, they vanished. "It seemed miraculous that they were never seen again," Luca wrote, "and as if it must signify something"—but just what, he did not say.

Less than a month after Savonarola's death, a 29-year-old Florentine named Niccolò Machiavelli started work as a civil servant for the republic. At first his duties did not amount to much, and the greater part of his day was spent on menial secretarial tasks, such as writing letters and compiling minutes of meetings.

But Machiavelli liked the job. For one thing, it was convenient to home. He worked on the top floor of the Palazzo della Signoria and lived nearby on the south bank of the Arno in the home of his father, Bernardo, a lawyer from an old family but of modest means. The young civil servant could count the number of steps to work: Fifty took him to the Ponte Vecchio, the stone bridge that spanned the river at its narrowest point, and about 100 more carried him on to the palace. But best of all, the job placed him near the center of Florentine political power, and Niccolò Machiavelli had an unquenchable passion for politics.

His intelligence and energy quickly won him greater responsibilities. First he became secretary to the city's executive committee for war and foreign affairs. This proved to be a lively spot at a time when armies were tramping up and down the Italian peninsula. Then he was sent on diplomatic missions to France, Germany, and the other city-states of Italy. Finally in 1502 he secured a job of real influence. That year a man named Piero Soderini was elected as the Signoria's gonfalonier of justice, normally a two-month position but now transformed into a lifetime post. Soderini chose Machiavelli as his most trusted adviser.

Machiavelli's major contribution in his new post was the establishment of a state militia. The unreliable professional mercenaries that had for so long fought Florence's wars were replaced by conscripts recruited from among the Tuscan peasantry. Under Machiavelli's command in 1509, this new militia helped restore to Florentine control the port city of Pisa.

In 1512, however, Machiavelli's 14-year career in politics came to an abrupt end. Florence at that time found itself caught between the forces of the pope's Holy League and his Spanish al-

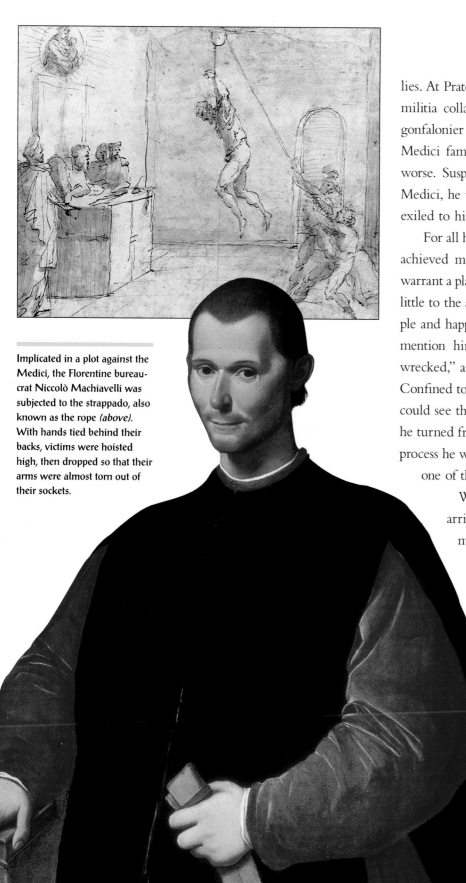

Implicated in a plot against the Medici, the Florentine bureaucrat Niccolò Machiavelli was subjected to the strappado, also known as the rope (above). With hands tied behind their backs, victims were hoisted high, then dropped so that their arms were almost torn out of their sockets.

lies. At Prato, a dozen miles northwest of Florence, Machiavelli's militia collapsed in the face of veteran Spanish warriors. The gonfalonier for life, Piero Soderini, fled into exile, and the Medici family returned to power. Machiavelli was fired—and worse. Suspected of involvement in a conspiracy against the Medici, he was arrested, tortured, and—although exonerated—exiled to his villa in the country.

For all his short-lived political influence, Machiavelli had not achieved major standing in Florence, certainly not enough to warrant a place in the history of the Renaissance. His name meant little to the average Florentine; that chronicler of important people and happenings, Luca Landucci, never saw fit to so much as mention him in his diary. But "after everything was totally wrecked," as Machiavelli put it, a remarkable thing happened. Confined to the old family estate in Percussina—from where he could see the dome of Florence's cathedral just 10 miles away—he turned from the practice of politics to writing about it. In the process he would make himself the father of political science and one of the greatest writers of Italian prose.

What occupied Machiavelli's thoughts when he first arrived at Percussina in the spring of 1513, however, was money. After losing his job with the government and posting a surety of 1,000 gold florins to guarantee that he would not leave the Florentine jurisdiction for a year, Machiavelli was virtually penniless. Some income came from leasing the family home in Florence, but not enough. By now he had a wife and a growing family to support. "I cannot stay here a long time," he wrote a friend, "without becoming contemptible through poverty."

Cash poor but land rich, Machiavelli owned an estate that had been in the family's hands for two cen-

A PLACE IN THE COUNTRY

The older or more prosperous Florentine families owned country estates such as the Villa di Collesalvetti *(below),* where they might spend several months a year to escape the heat and pressures of urban life. Judging from the fields, barns, and peasant huts in the foreground, Collesalvetti was also a farm, producing food and income for the owners, who sold the surplus.

The most profitable products were oil and wine, and Tuscany was a patchwork of olive groves and grape arbors *(left).* Grain, fruit, and nuts were also grown. Most laborers worked on a tenant-farming basis, sharing costs, crops, and even oversight of the farm with owners. By supplying food to Florence, which in turn safeguarded the peasantry from war and political strife, villas like Collesalvetti helped forge the strong bond that existed between urban and rural Tuscans.

turies. It included much of the hilltop hamlet of Sant'Andrea, on the postal road to Rome, with its inn, butcher shop, and half-dozen houses. His fields and woodlands produced crops and lumber that he shared with his tenants. On thin and rocky soil nourished by too little rain, the tenants raised pigs, a few cows, corn and barley, fruits and nuts, and enough olives annually to yield perhaps a dozen barrels of oil and sufficient grapes for 40 or so barrels of wine.

With much of his time taken up running the estate, Machiavelli eventually settled into a daily routine—one very different from what he'd been used to in Florence. He rose at dawn and went to his forest to inspect the work of the woodcutters, who, he complained, "have always some troubles to tell me, either of their own or their neighbors." Then he might head off to inspect a spring on his estate or pay a visit to his bird-snaring enclosure. With him he usually carried a book—"Dante, Petrarch, or one of the minor poets, such as Tibullus or Ovid." As opportunities presented themselves throughout the day, he would leaf through a few pages, reading about the lives of these authors and "of their amorous passions and of their loves." Fondly, he would recall his own youth in Florence and the young women he had been acquainted with there.

But even at the estate, far from the glitter of Florence, the married Machiavelli continued to have affairs. "Cupid's nets still enthrall me," he wrote to a friend. "My whole mind is bent on love, for which I give Venus thanks." Within a year of moving to the country, he would fall in love with a neighbor, "so gracious, so delicate, so noble." Only such an enticing dalliance, which required a great deal of stealth to maintain secretly in this rural area, could compete with his ardor for politics. But he wrote a friend that it was worth it: "I believe, believed, and always shall believe that what Boccaccio says is true—that it is better to do and regret than not to do and regret."

For lunch Machiavelli returned home to a meager meal with his family. "I swallow whatever fare this poor little place of mine, and my slender patrimony, can afford me," he lamented. Much of the rest of the day he would spend at the local inn, chatting with passersby and seeking news of the outside world. With the innkeeper and local tradesmen, he played cards or dice, idling away the hours. The gambling was accompanied by "much exchange of bad language" and wrangling over pennies. Thus frittering away the day "steeped in this degradation," he felt his "wits grow moldy" and vented his rage "at the indignity of fate."

At dusk, however, Machiavelli's other life began. After returning from the inn, he would head for the writing room on the ground floor of his home. In the passageway that led to the room, a closet on the left contained a stone washbowl where he could clean his hands and face. On the right was another closet, from which he took a fresh change of clothing. Shucking off his mud-stained garments and footwear that smelled of poultry and hay, he put on courtly robes and slippers of the type he would have worn on one of his former diplomatic missions to the palaces of nobles. Then he crossed the threshold into the room, lighted a lamp, and sat down at his writing table. Letting his imagination run free, he entered "the ancient courts of ancient men."

There, for the next four hours, Machiavelli conversed with the great thinkers of the past, such as Livy, Tacitus, and Aristotle. He talked with them about his favorite subject, politics. "It is necessary that I reason about the state," he wrote. And as he gently probed their motivations and made notes from their replies, his mind escaped the straitened circumstances of his exile. "I feel no weariness. I forget every trouble. I do not fear poverty. Death does not dismay me."

From these nightly conversations—and his own experiences in government—Machiavelli produced in 1513 a short treatise on the art of government. Titled *The Prince,* it was a guidebook on how to create and maintain a powerful state. Unlike the authors of other such books, Machiavelli refused to preach sermons about morals and ethics; he had lived through the strife of the Savonarola era and knew that was not enough. He wrote not about what a ruler should do morally but what he had to do to survive. And what that prince had to do was to practice expediency, cunning, deceit, hypocrisy, intrigue, ruthlessness, cruelty, and if necessary, murder.

As his model for this new prince, Machiavelli selected one of the most notorious rulers of Renaissance Italy, Cesare Borgia. Cesare was the son of Rodrigo Borgia, the flamboyant Spaniard who became Pope Alexander VI and helped bring down Savonarola. While most popes tried to cover up their illicit sexual liaisons by referring to their offspring as nephews, Alexander openly boasted about his many children. He even had a portrait of his official mistress, dressed as the Virgin Mary, painted over the door of his bedchamber. Alexander wanted to reestablish Rome's control over the rebellious Papal States, and he selected Cesare as the man to do it. To finance his military campaigns, the pope resorted to the usual tactics of selling high offices and taking over the estates of dead bishops and cardinals—some of whom, it was said, he hastened along with poison.

His son Cesare was just 24 years old in 1500 when he undertook his first campaigns in central Italy. Tall and handsome, he was so strong he could twist a horseshoe with his hands or decapitate a bull with a single stroke of his sword. He usually wore a simple black doublet under a light suit of armor and a large beret with a dashing white plume, though he could also ornament himself outrageously with pearl-studded boots edged in gold and his horse with solid-silver horseshoes.

Alexander had made him a cardinal at age 17, but Cesare had renounced the cardinal's red hat in order to cut a swath in the larger world. Women loved him but learned not to expect much from him. He married a cousin of the king of France, left her pregnant, and never went back to her. He was accused of raping the famed warrior-ruler of Imola and Forlì, Caterina Sforza. And

he may have murdered his older brother and almost certainly killed the second husband of his sister, Lucrezia.

In just three years young Borgia and his armies subdued the rulers of a dozen towns of the Romagna, the largest province of the Papal States. He became one of the most powerful men in Italy, governor of a realm exceeded in size only by the kingdom of Naples. As a military commander, he proved to be a mediocre tactician but a genius at trickery and intrigue who could strike terror into the hearts of ordinary men. The apothecary Luca Landucci said that news of one of Borgia's brutal episodes made him "tremble with the fear of God on hearing it." But for Machiavelli, the ends justified the means: "He was considered cruel; nevertheless his cruelty reconciled all the Romagna, unified it, and restored it to peace and loyalty."

Machiavelli's enchantment with Cesare Borgia stemmed from a series of meetings back in 1502. The government of Florence had sent Machiavelli to negotiate with Borgia, who was demanding that the city-state pay him protection in order to maintain friendly relations. Borgia received him with typical dramatic flair: in his tent at night by the light of a single flickering candle while clad in black from head to foot. Machiavelli spent three months with him, wide eyed with wonder at the resolute will to power of this man of action six years his junior. "This lord is very splendid and magnificent," Machiavelli wrote to his superiors, "and so spirited at arms that there is no great thing that does not seem to him small."

Machiavelli liked Borgia's policy of relying on local conscripts rather than foreign mercenaries, and he borrowed the practice for Florence. But it was the young tyrant's knack for treachery that impressed him most of all. He would, for example, allow a deputy to tyrannize his subjects and then have the deputy murdered to show the people that he himself was a just ruler. Machiavelli also admired the way Borgia dealt with four men suspected of hatching a conspiracy against him: With great

In the study at his country villa at Percussina, Machiavelli composed his famous—or infamous—treatise on the principles of effective governance, *The Prince.* The writing life agreed with Machiavelli; many distinguished works followed, including *La Mandragola,* a popular farce about Renaissance morals.

cordiality, he invited them to a conciliatory meeting, then seized them and had them put to death.

A taut writing style laced with epigrams characterized *The Prince.* "I have not decorated this work with blown-up cadences or turgid and magnificent words or any other preciousness or extrinsic ornamentation," Machiavelli asserted. What he neglected to mention was his penchant for bold, sweeping statements and startling omissions. He failed to point out, for instance, that Borgia's success depended in large part on the power of his father. After Pope Alexander died in 1503 of a malarial infection, young Borgia's budding empire quickly crumbled. Borgia was imprisoned for a while in the family's native Spain and was killed in battle in 1507.

In the final chapter of *The Prince,* Machiavelli tried to explain some of the apparent

schemes; they did not respond to his letters, and his book—which Machiavelli had dedicated to a nephew of the new pope—circulated only in manuscript form.

After 1513 Machiavelli's evenings in his writing room were concerned with ever more imaginative endeavors as he turned to fiction and plays. In 1520 his stage comedy *Mandragola* was performed before Pope Leo in Rome with great success. The play, with its satirical seductions and corrupt priest, so pleased the Medici pope that he arranged employment for Machiavelli as a writer. The assignment, a history of Florence, forced Machiavelli to confront his own republican conscience; he had to maintain a delicate balance between his own intellectual convictions and the flattery demanded by his patrons. This he accomplished in truly Machiavellian fashion, by praising the personal qualities of old Cosi-

"*I*taly is ready and willing to follow a banner, if only someone will raise it."

inconsistencies in this cynical handbook for tyrants, written by a man who had served republican Florence with selfless devotion. Machiavelli believed Italy's troubles with foreign invaders stemmed from its lack of unity. Only a strong leader, even a tyrant, could impose that unity on the peninsula's fragmented city-states. "Italy is ready and willing to follow a banner," he wrote, "if only someone will raise it."

Machiavelli hoped that the Medici would raise that banner—and that the family that had driven him out of government would recall him to help unify Italy. The Medici now ruled two former enemies in the unified state he envisioned: Florence and the Papal States, where Lorenzo's son Giovanni was now Pope Leo X. But the Medici seemed uninterested in his

mo de' Medici and his grandson Lorenzo rather than their autocratic methods of ruling Florence.

His successful completion of the history in 1525 led to further ironies. He was assigned the task of fortifying the walls of Florence—just in time for his Medici masters to be deposed once again. Machiavelli rejoiced at the departure of the family and immediately applied to the new republican government for his old job as secretary of the committee for war and foreign affairs. Ironically, on June 10, 1527, he was turned down because of his association with the Medici. Twelve days later Niccolò Machiavelli died, in poverty and dejection and with no inkling that his name would survive, unjustly perhaps, as a synonym for cynical political expediency.

SUMPTUOUS CELEBRATIONS

As Italian cities grew wealthier, they competed with one another in hosting lavish festivals. Although many of these celebrations marked church holy days, the extravagant festivities often signified civic pride more than religious fervor. To honor their patron saint, welcome a foreign dignitary, or glorify a noble family, Italian cities went all out, putting on fireworks displays—such as the one depicted at right marking the feast day of John the Baptist in Florence—and staging triumphal processions, horse races, religious dramas, mock battles, feasts, dances, poetry contests, masquerades, and jousts and tournaments.

The cities themselves provided the backdrop for these activities. Their narrow, winding streets determined the pace and rhythm of a procession or race, and the wide piazzas—surrounded by tall buildings with windows and balconies accommodating the many spectators—provided the perfect setting for the events that the city fathers hoped would make their festival more spectacular than any other.

VENICE: HOMAGE TO THE SEA

Pope Alexander III offers Doge Sebastiano Ziani a gold ring to thank him for helping to secure peace in 1177 *(left)*. A replica of the ring later became part of the annual ritual in which the doge—below, under a golden umbrella and followed by red-robed clerics—is rowed out to the Adriatic on his ceremonial barge, where he reaffirms the city's bond with the sea.

Because Venetians depended upon the sea for their livelihood, the city's most important festival included a symbolic marriage between the republic of Venice and the Adriatic Sea. The 15-day feast marked the anniversary of the occasion in 998 when Doge Pietro Orseolo II sailed off to rescue the country of Dalmatia from pirates' rule. The celebration took place in the spring, coinciding with Ascension Day, so the Sposalizio del Mare—or Marriage of the Sea— incorporated religious elements as well.

On Ascension Day, the doge would first attend Mass. Afterward, along with the patriarch of Constantinople and other dignitaries, he boarded his *bucintoro,* or ceremonial barge. Hundreds of private boats followed the barge out toward the sea, where the patriarch blessed the water and a gold ring, which the doge then dropped overboard, saying, "We espouse thee, O sea, as a sign of true and perpetual dominion."

FLORENCE: FEAST OF SAINT JOHN THE BAPTIST

"When springtime comes," wrote Florentine merchant Gregorio Dati in 1410, "every Florentine begins thinking about celebrating a beautiful feast of San Giovanni." Indeed, weeks before the start of the summer festival honoring John the Baptist, the patron saint of Florence, workers draped houses and grandstands along the processional route with rich cloth and sewed an enormous canopy—or "heaven"—over the entire Piazza di San Giovanni. There, according to one observer, the city's merchants would put out on display "whatever precious things they have," such as jewels, armor, and reliquaries, "for the greater honor of the city."

Two days before the feast day, floats depicting biblical scenes paraded through the streets, and on June 23, clergymen in "vestments of gold and of silk and of embroidered figures" processed through town, beginning and ending at the cathedral. In the evening, two men from each household in the city carried torches to the baptistery dedicated to Saint John, and in the glow of perhaps 20,000 such torches, fireworks exploded over the piazza.

The following morning, June 24, the bishop said Mass and accepted offerings in Saint John's name. Then came the main event—the *palio,* a horse race so called after the bolt of precious cloth that was to be the winner's prize.

Beneath a canopy decorated with guild insignia and the emblematic lily of Florence *(below)*, magistrates and others arrive at the baptistery raising high their *palii*—silk banners—as offerings to Saint John the Baptist on his feast day. In the scene at right, a horse and rider go down during the running of the palio through the streets of Florence.

On this ceremonial shield—carried in processions during celebrations such as the Feast of Saint John—David, the symbol of Florence, proclaims his triumph over the mighty Goliath, whose head lies at David's feet.

107

SIENA: THE ASSUMPTION OF THE VIRGIN

The Feast of the Assumption, celebrated on August 15, commemorates the Virgin Mary's ascent into heaven, and in Renaissance Siena, where Mary was revered as the city's patron, it was the occasion for a grand festival. Each city district contributed a float for the opening procession, along with flag bearers, pages, and drummers in distinctive costumes. Viewed by thousands of spectators lining the streets or watching from windows and rooftops overlooking the Piazza del Campo, the procession set the stage for the main event: the palio, in which horses from the city districts were blessed by the church and then raced around the piazza.

The residents of Siena valued this feast day so highly that they celebrated it even when they were under threat of invasion. The annual celebration took place on schedule during wartime in 1474—with a fireworks display fueled by gunpowder taken from military stores.

Spectators throng Siena's Piazza del Campo to watch as costumed ambassadors from each city ward march behind wheeled floats depicting their district's animal emblem. Among the animals shown are a snail, an elephant, a cow, a dragon, and a unicorn *(right)*. Below, city officials offer the keys to Siena to the Virgin Mary in a symbolic rendering of the feast day.

Three masked revelers carrying a basket of perfume-filled eggs prepare to pelt each other as they stroll past street jugglers and a costumed couple in this Venice carnival scene.

In the painting below, carnival floats represent the triumphs of Love, Chastity, and Death. During the Florentine carnival of 1512, a giant figure of Death rode a black-draped float embellished with skeletons, reminding revelers that all must one day die.

A WORLD TURNED UPSIDE DOWN

Masked singers led by a nobleman believed to be Lorenzo de' Medici serenade the ladies of Florence *(above)*.

"Youths and maids, enjoy today; / Nought ye know about tomorrow," went the refrain of a popular poem, penned in the 1480s by Lorenzo de' Medici, encapsulating the exuberant spirit of carnival. In a burst of excess before the austerity of Lent—a 40-day religious observance in which the faithful abstained from eating meat—carnival turned the everyday world topsy-turvy.

The traditions of carnival—feasting, merrymaking, and temporarily ignoring social distinctions and rules—had their roots in pre-Christian festivals to celebrate the end of the agricultural year. By the time of the Renaissance, city dwellers had expanded on the ancient themes. They ate rich foods, played pranks, staged jousts, sang and danced, mocked authority, and wore masks and disguises. Nobles dressed like peasants, men wore women's clothing, and vice versa. Young boys in Florence staged rock fights, lit bonfires, and blocked street corners to extort money from passersby. And in Venice, daredevils walked tightropes strung from boats in the lagoon to the bell tower in the Piazza San Marco. All over Italy, it seemed, a spirit of chaos reigned supreme.

theses—against all comers, even, if necessary, paying the travel expenses of any hopeful challenger who cared to meet him in Rome early in 1487.

Needing time to prepare for this showdown with his fellow scholars, Pico traveled to Rome in the fall of 1486 and found the place as unattractive as he remembered it from earlier visits. Indeed, accustomed as he was to Florence, he could hardly be blamed for thinking that more than distance separated the two cities. It was true that both were cities of towers, and neither had streets that were anything more than cramped. But where Florence had in recent decades assumed a grace that was as much atmospheric as aesthetic, Rome remained a collection of overgrown medieval villages, and only in its ruins could anything of its former grandeur be seen. Even there, rusticity ruled, with cows grazing in the Forum, horses around the Trajan's Column, and sheep on most of the Seven Hills. Everywhere, as Pico's nose could attest, the place smelled less like a city than a barnyard.

Equally pervasive in Rome was the presence of the church, although the successors of one midcentury pope had not yet taken to heart his deathbed request that "noble edifices" were needed for "the exaltation of the chair of St. Peter." But if the church's influence was not yet apparent in Rome's architecture, its presence was felt in the city's administration. Even for those practiced in such skills, going against the papal court was quite a challenge. And for a brash and dangerously reckless amateur like Pico, the publication of his 900 theses in December 1486 marked a fateful step onto ground that was decidedly unsteady, and where his footing was precariously insecure.

Pico had anticipated that the publication of his work would ensure a large turnout for his proposed symposium. But to his disappointment, January 1487 passed without a single scholar accepting Pico's challenge to debate his theses. Left unread, therefore, was the speech he had written for the occasion, his *Oration, on the Dignity of Man,* in which he depicted humans as unique in "the universal chain of Being." Of all the earth's creatures, Pico claimed, only man could affect his destiny, his free will governing whether he sank to the level of brutes or rose to the level of the divine. Through contemplation, by suppression of human passions, by dint of the will that was not given to animals, the philosopher would have informed his audience, those who "long with love for the Creator" shall be illuminated, their souls perfected, their "aspiration to the angelic way of life" achieved.

The speech had no chance of offending the Vatican, though, since nobody there had the opportunity to read it until years after Pico's death. Pope Innocent VIII and his minions did read the 900 theses, however, and the reaction was predictable: Pico's espousal of magic and mysticism was questionable enough, but his notion that even the most mortal of mortal sins did not merit eternal damnation smelled of heresy. And where there was smoke, as Innocent himself intimated, there might yet be fire. "This young man," warned the pontiff, "wants someone to burn him some day."

Pico's timing could not have been worse. The church, hardly open minded in its relationships with freethinkers, had recently given the Inquisition the license to show heretics the error of their ways. Events moved swiftly. In March 1487 a papal commission condemned as heretical seven of Pico's theses and branded six more of questionable orthodoxy. Pico responded, impulsively again, with a written defense that soon prompted an official investigation for heresy. The verdict: Pico's theses, ruled the Vatican, "savor of heresy" and "repeat the errors of pagan philosophers"; they "are inimical to the Catholic faith."

Still in Rome, Pico may have reasoned that it was safer to be among enemies than to attempt to outrun them. But with the public announcement of his condemnation in December, he hesitated, pondered his options, hesitated some more, and then dart-

A female personification of the moon astride the zodiac sign of Cancer–which ruled the ocean and ports–accompanies seafarers in this illustration from *De Sphaera*, an astrological manuscript illuminated around 1450. Belief in astrology was widespread during the Renaissance: Universities taught it; humanists studied its ancient roots; astrologers divined at every court; and sailors, doctors, popes, and brides all consulted horoscopes.

ed for cover, fleeing for Paris even as the papal order for his arrest made its way to the grand inquisitor Torquemada. Not long afterward, he was arrested and imprisoned in France.

News of Pico's arrest sparked an outcry from the French court and from his admirers at the Sorbonne, but to no avail. In his cell near Paris, the prisoner listened for the scuff of boots and the scrape of a key that might signal his release, only to see hope rewarded with what passed for a meal. Days, measured in his own pacing, swirled into nights enlivened by the skitter of rats across the stone floor, until Pico no longer counted the hours or the days or dared to allow himself the hope of freedom. Then, without warning, about a month after his capture, the heavy door swung open to the squeak of unoiled hinges, and the prisoner was ordered from his cell.

To his surprise, Pico was free. Once again, his powerful Medici friends had come to his rescue and had secured his release, and he made his way back to Florence. But there was a seriousness now that had been absent before in the young man, a wariness, a somber resignation. And while Pico was absolved by the new pope, Alexander VI, in 1493, the pardon itself did little to brighten the forgiven heretic's outlook on life.

In contrast to his former life, Pico became more ascetic in his habits. He would, he now decided, live like the monk he had almost already become. In short order he burned the volumes of love poetry he had penned, wrote a book condemning the astrology he had once defended, sold his title, and donated his fortune to provide dowries for indigent girls. By late 1494, when he stood in the crowded church of San Marco and felt his skin crawl and his hair stand on end as the fiery priest Girolamo Savonarola prophesied doom from the pulpit, all that remained for Pico della Mirandola was to renounce the world at last and take his vows as a Dominican.

But time was about to run out, as much for Florence as for Pico. On November 17, 1494, King Charles VIII of France, at the head of a great invading army, trotted on horseback through the Porta San Frediano and made Florence his own. That very day, along one of the city's serpentine streets, in rooms swept clean of all worldliness, the 31-year-old Giovanni Pico della Mirandola lay in bed with a deadly fever, his hopes of becoming a Dominican ebbing on the tide of his dying breath.

Charles VIII's armed arrival in Florence came in direct response to an invitation from Ludovico Sforza, the scheming duke of Milan, who had hoped that the French army would keep his own enemies at bay while he secured his claim to power in Milan. The plan worked, to a point, until Sforza realized that his French guest was in no hurry to leave Italy. Only when he was sped on his way by a combined Italian army, including Sforza's Milanese forces, did Charles return to France, where he died three years later.

Unfortunately for Sforza, Charles's successor, Louis XII, took it upon himself to avenge his predecessor's rough treatment in Italy. In August 1499 the French returned to the peninsula, uninvited and no less belligerent than on their earlier visit, and this time with their sights set on Milan. Sforza, unable to raise a large enough army to save his duchy, decided to save himself instead and fled north across the Alps, leaving his subjects to fend for themselves with the rampaging French.

Hurrying through the rubbled streets of Milan, the belled sleeves of his *lucco,* or gown, rippling in the morning breeze, one of Sforza's erstwhile subjects, the maestro Leonardo da Vinci, could imagine himself in better circumstances than these, with his adopted city in enemy hands and his once powerful patron on the run. How odd, too, he might have thought, that he had first arrived in Milan from Florence, what was it now, 16 or 17 years ago, expecting to design bridges for Duke Ludovico Sforza, to build weapons, to install the kind of defenses no enemy could ever breach. But the duke had never given his proposals a passing thought. And where was the farsighted Ludovico now? Hightailing it for the city of Innsbruck, Leonardo thought derisively, his long stride stepping off the last few yards to the monastery of Santa Maria delle Grazie.

Entering the building with barely a word to the monk at the gate, Leonardo followed a familiar corridor, then turned a corner and slipped into the refectory. "Thanks be to God," he heard himself say out loud, stopping in his tracks as his gaze met the far wall.

THE AGE OF EXPLORATION

Genoa's Christopher Columbus *(below)* typified the age in his bold optimism and tenacity. Part dreamer, part missionary, and part soldier of fortune, the skilled mariner taught himself Latin in order to study geographical texts. Convinced, like others, that the earth was round, he sailed west to reach the East, where he hoped to establish a center of trade. He underestimated the earth's size, however, landing not in Japan but in the Bahamas.

Nevertheless, Columbus's discovery was the talk of Europe. Soon others were exploring not just the New World but the whole world. Within 30 years Vasco Núñez de Balboa had sighted the Pacific Ocean, Vasco da Gama had discovered a route to India, and Ferdinand Magellan's crew had circled the globe.

The painting was safe. There were rumors, nothing more, but worrisome nonetheless—that the invaders intended to take *The Last Supper* back to France, even if it meant dismantling the wall on which the mural had been painted. But the painting was safe. "Thanks be to God." He whispered it this time. "It's safe."

Craning his head, Leonardo stared at his work, his eyes finding fault where nobody else's would. It always seemed to him that he could do more, although it bothered him, too, that some—even the prior of this very monastery—thought that his perfectionism kept him from completing his works.

If the truth were told, Leonardo would have countered, his long tenure in Milan was not without accomplishments. He had, after all, completed the *Virgin of the Rocks,* and he had devoted years to the *gran cavallo,* that immense statue of a prancing horse, a monument, as he told the duke, to "the illustrious house of Sforza." That the statue had never been cast was due entirely to Ludovico, who needed the bronze for cannons. Nor was it his fault, Leonardo would have argued, that he had been forced by Ludovico to spend so much time designing costumes and devising elaborate stage shows for court pageants and even, heaven forbid, fashioning corsets for the duke's teenage bride.

Leonardo took a few steps backward and looked up again at *The Last Supper.* Three long years of work, he thought, often from sunrise until dark, sometimes painting for hours on end without stopping to eat or drink. At other times, his hand had never touched a brush, for hours and even days at a stretch, as he struggled with some nuance of composition or technique; then, having resolved the issue in his mind, he would add a hurried

Leonardo da Vinci's *Last Supper* captures the moment when the apostles, having heard Christ's prediction of betrayal, react in shock, each asking, "Lord, is it I?" Judas alone pulls back, clutching a bag of silver. Painted on a wall of the refectory of Santa Maria delle Grazie, where the resident friars ate meals, the painting reminded the monks, as they broke bread, of the first Holy Communion.

Leonardo took his surname from Vinci *(right)*, the small Tuscan town near which he was born. In this rolling countryside, the artist-scientist spent his childhood exploring nature and its forces. "It is important to go straight to nature," he would later say, "rather than to the masters who have learned from her."

stroke or two to the painting and immediately call it a day.

The process—no, the ordeal—had been enough to drive the monastery's prior up the wall, and the frustrated monk had gone so far as to complain to Duke Ludovico about the painter's apparent inactivity. "Men of genius do most when they work least," Leonardo remembered telling the duke in his own defense, succinctly distinguishing the day-laboring craftsman from the artist answerable only to himself and to inspiration. Luckily, recalled Leonardo, Ludovico had sided with this particular artist, the duke even chuckling to himself when Leonardo threatened to use the petty-minded prior as the model for the head of Judas.

At that moment, the shuffle of approaching sandals shook Leonardo from his reverie, and he looked around for the small stove that had been his excuse to visit the refectory. Now that he had made up his mind to leave Milan—the looting had been bad enough after the French first occupied the city, but the recent killings had been all too much to bear—he was intent on collecting his belongings. The smaller things would go with him; the larger, like the stove, he would sell for needed cash.

A quick search of the room failed to produce the stove. Just as well, Leonardo thought to himself, as a line of cowled monks slithered into the room behind their prior. The stove was nothing so much as a bad memory. He had used it to help take the dampness out of the room while he was working on *The Last Supper.* And dampness, he reflected, had been the bane of his days here. It was largely his own fault, he knew. After all, it was he who had opted for tempera—in which pigments mixed with an

egg-yolk medium are brushed onto a dry wall—over the safer fresco, whereby water-based paint is hurriedly applied to a fresh finishing coat of plaster before the plaster can dry. And it was he who had chosen to brush the tempera onto an experimental primer of pitch and mastic. Nothing had worked, however, not the stove and not the primer, and the effects were already sadly apparent in patches of mottled paint.

With a last look at the painting and a nod in the direction of the expressionless prior, standing, fittingly, at the long table beneath the figure of Judas, Leonardo slipped quietly from the refectory. Pulling his lucco tighter around him, he stepped from the gate and out into the cold December air.

In preparation for his departure from Milan, Leonardo had already forwarded most of his savings to Florence's Monte di Pietà bank. Three boxes—stuffed with books and bed linens, clothing, paints and paper, and a handful of lily and watermelon seeds—had also been dispatched separately by mule and driver. He himself would take a more meandering route south, stopping in Mantua, where there was at least the prospect of work from Duke Ludovico's tenacious sister-in-law, Isabella d'Este, and a stopover in Venice before striking out for Florence.

For Leonardo, transitions like this were as much a time for reflection as they were for anticipation, and he had indeed come far in his 47 years. It was clear to him, however, that he would never outrun the illegitimacy of his birth, the success and reputation of his notary father notwithstanding. Renaissance society might ignore, but would never countenance, his father's liaison with the gentle but humbly born Caterina, and the price of Leonardo's illegitimacy had been alienation from conventional professional paths.

How long ago it now seemed since he had made the day's journey to Florence to begin his apprenticeship to the master Andrea del Verrocchio, leaving behind the fissured hills, the shin-gled vineyards, and crystalline air of tiny Vinci. In his teens, dark haired and almost pretty, he had appeared at Verrocchio's bottega on the Via de Agnolo after first running the usual street slalom of children, dogs, pigs, and chickens. Ducking under the awning that sheltered the doorway of the workshop and stepping inside, Leonardo found himself in a single room, its walls whitewashed and hung with sketches, the room itself strewn with supplies and a surprising variety of works in progress. For like other such bottegas, Verrocchio's workshop was less a studio than a factory, and its output included not just paintings and sculpture, but candelabra, armor, and cast-metal bells.

As part of his own training, Leonardo would have taken on any number of increasingly greater responsibilities, from cleaning paintbrushes and sweeping the floor at the end of the day's work to mixing pigments for a painting and rough-cutting stone for a sculpture. Gradually, he would have been allowed to brush in backgrounds or to complete whole sections of a work on his own, continually refining his skills by observation and experience, until by the end of his apprenticeship he would have achieved the mastery that entitled him to be called maestro.

For Leonardo, that day had come in 1472, six years after his arrival in Florence, when his name was inked into the "Red book of the debtors and creditors of St. Luke," the roster of the guild that included apothecaries and spice dealers—purveyors of medicines and pigments, respectively—and their bread-and-butter customers, physicians and artists. But although he was then qualified to set up a shop of his own, Leonardo chose to stay on with Verrocchio for several more years, perhaps unwilling to take on the burdens of an independent maestro when he was still needed in his master's shop.

Looking back, he recalled the many hours he had already devoted to his various pursuits. Optics, botany, mechanics, music, hydraulics, weaponry, astronomy, city planning—there was little that didn't interest him. And no science ranked higher in his

THE GENIUS OF LEONARDO DA VINCI

Leonardo da Vinci's brilliance was not confined to his masterpieces of painting. It is also evident in the notebooks in which he recorded visionary inventions and observations of natural phenomena. Leonardo began sketching mechanical systems and devices while at the Sforza court in Milan. Like other artists of the day, he had to master engineering and architecture in order to design a variety of projects, from canals, bridges, streets, and buildings to floats and costumes for court pageants. But what began as professional necessity soon turned into pure scientific research. With restless curiosity, he deconstructed machines, animals, and plants, analyzing the principles by which they worked.

By the time he died in 1519, Leonardo had filled more than 5,000 notebook pages with a patchwork of intricate drawings annotated in backward script, legible only in a mirror. Some sketches were pure flights of fancy—allegorical animals, costumes, caricatures; others were serious studies of flight, including a prototype of a helicopter.

Although the mechanical loom may be the sole invention he saw realized, Leonardo envisioned other things that did not become possible until centuries later, among them the parachute, crank elevator, bicycle, military tank, machine gun, submarine, diving suit, and an inflatable life jacket. Moreover, his analytical drawings of human anatomy became the basis of improved medical texts and marked the beginning of comparative anatomy.

SELF-PORTRAIT, CA. 1512

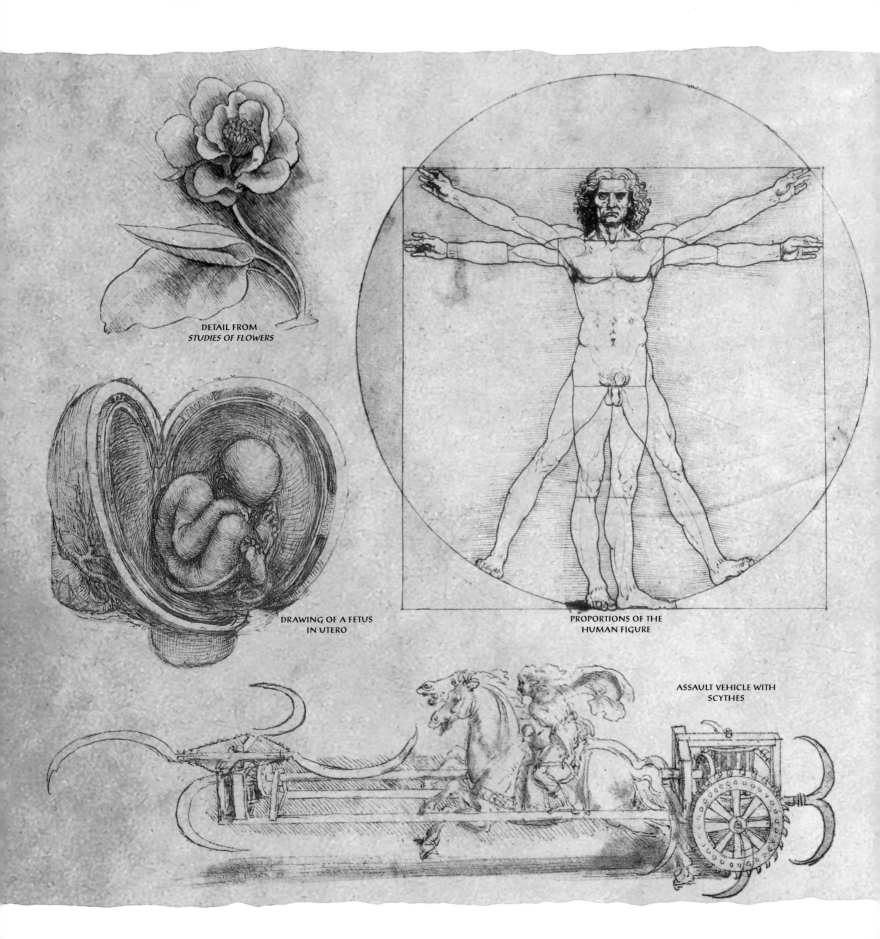

DETAIL FROM
STUDIES OF FLOWERS

DRAWING OF A FETUS
IN UTERO

PROPORTIONS OF THE
HUMAN FIGURE

ASSAULT VEHICLE WITH
SCYTHES

LIFE PRESERVER

THE AERODYNAMICS OF
VERTICAL FLIGHT

A WOODEN WING OPERATED
BY A HAND CRANK

estimation than mathematics, as he once confided to his notebook. "He who does not know the supreme certainty of mathematics," he scrawled, "is wallowing in confusion." Why, even the marvels of the human body could be understood as nothing more than the workings of a wondrous machine—a machine governable, like all machines, by the principles of mechanics and the immutable laws of mathematics.

"Observation is everything," he might have told his own pupils. "Start with what you can see, and learn from what you can discover." Such a philosophy had always guided his own discoveries, as his anatomical drawings so clearly showed; "my gift to mankind," Leonardo would call those drawings, the result of his candlelit dissections of more than 30 cadavers. His later interest in flight, too, would have its starting point in his observations of birds in motion, in his explorations of the intricacies of their anatomy, and in his application of that knowledge to a machine that would mimic a bird's motion. After all, as Leonardo characteristically deduced, a bird was nothing more than "an instrument operating through mathematical laws."

For all his faith in the laws of mathematics, Leonardo must have wondered at times if those laws, or any laws at all for that matter, applied to the artful Salai, the 19-year-old he had taken into his household some

nine years earlier, and who was even now accompanying the maestro to Florence. The word Salai meant "limb of Satan," and it was an appropriate nickname for an urchin given to pinching purses and anything else that could be sold for cash. And time, to Leonardo's disappointment, had done little to change Salai. Still, for all his devilish temperament, the youth had the face of an angel, and Leonardo was happy to have his company.

Stopping off in Mantua, Leonardo allowed the marchioness Isabella d'Este to give him a tour of her *studiolo*, the private apartments that formed her personal museum. The insistent Isabella, her arm on Leonardo's, had already let it be known that she wouldn't be happy until he had painted her portrait. Leonardo, in need of a patron but wary of the marchioness's outward charm, took care to humor her. He would see what he could do, he told her, although he couldn't predict how long he would stay in Mantua.

Leonardo was not unaware of Isabella's reputation for lording it over the beneficiaries of her patronage. She had, after all, already taken Bellini to court for his failure to produce a painting done to her exacting specifications. With his distaste for deadlines and his need for creative freedom, Leonardo, like an increasing number of artists, could never abide so short a leash. He would do something less than a full-blown portrait of Isabella, a drawing, enough to satisfy her without offending her. And then he must be on his way. "When you are alone," he reminded himself, "you are entirely your own."

With Salai in tow, Leonardo soon left Mantua and pointed himself in the direction of Venice. He stayed only long enough to draw up plans to drown a valley—and with it a Turkish army that was threatening the city. The Venetian government, however, was no more appreciative of his military stratagems than Duke Ludovico had been. Taking to the road again, Leonardo set out for Florence in April 1500.

Having just turned 48, his hair graying, the corners of his mouth pleated with middle age, Leonardo arrived in Florence still between patrons. Fortunately, he had his savings to fall back on. Moreover, he was now in a city where commissions were more abundant than artists, thanks to the emergence of a thriving middle class with money to spend on works of art and building projects. That many of these commissions not only paid a stipend but also provided for room and board was all the more welcome.

Leonardo immediately put out the word that he was available for work and soon lined up a project—and lodgings—at the monastery of the Annunziata, where he was hired to do a painting for the high altar. Leonardo quickly settled in at his new address. But much to the concern of the resident monks, he did no painting—for days and weeks and then months on end—occupying himself instead with his beloved mathematics and

THE ITALIAN WAY OF WAR

When his Florentine army routed the Sienese at the Battle of San Romano in 1432 *(below)*, Captain General Niccolò da Tolentino was the toast of Florence. Yet one local politician, Alamanno Salviati, could muster nothing but contempt for Tolentino. "In general all men of his occupation disgust me," wrote Salviati, to whom the captain general was merely a mercenary, a soldier who was paid to fight.

But even Salviati knew that Florence needed mercenaries. War was a fact of life in Renaissance Italy. When not defending against foreign invasion, the in-dependent city-states that checkered the peninsula were fighting each other for control of limited territory, subjects, and trade. Rather than sacrifice their male citizens to endless battle, most city-states relied on hired armies.

Italy's early mercenaries had merited fear and loathing because during periods when they were unemployed, they tend-ed to turn outlaw. In the 15th century, however, these roving bands had large-ly become a thing of the past, to be re-placed by organized mercenary compa-nies led by professional captains like Tolentino. Captains signed formal con-tracts to provide services for city-states, and it was ill advised to betray one's employer. A city-state could fine or fire a captain for breach of contract and might even attempt to execute him for severe treachery.

But captains both loyal and talented were often rewarded with land, citizen-ship, and elevation to the nobility. Such treatment helped to domesticate the mercenary elite, so much so that during the 16th century they were primed to give up their freelance status and be-come soldiers in the permanent employ of individual states.

geometry. The poor monks, their patience tried, found themselves wishing that the artist originally contracted to do the job, Filippino Lippi, had been less courteous and had not withdrawn from the deal in deference to the great Leonardo.

In keeping with the belief that creativity could not be hurried, Leonardo, to all appearances, continued to dither away. "He seems to live for the day only," grumbled Fra Pietro da Novellara, writing to no less interested a correspondent than Isabella d'Este, herself still waiting for her portrait to be finished in color. Ten days later Fra Pietro, relaying information he had pried from Salai, told a disappointed Isabella that Leonardo's "mathematical experiments have absorbed his thoughts so entirely that he cannot bear the sight of a paintbrush."

When it came to the marchioness, Leonardo had every reason to avoid his paintbrushes, as he had no intention of completing the portrait. The monks were another matter, though, and in due course he set to work on a preliminary sketch, or cartoon, of the Virgin, her mother, Saint Anne, and the infant Christ.

"I wish to work miracles," a younger Leonardo had once confided to his notebook, and as he worked to achieve just the right balance of light and shadow, to endow the faces in the drawing with what he called *il concetto dell' anima*—"the idea of spirit"—something in his older self told him that he was, in a way, performing a miracle. Certainly, his employers believed it, so much so that when the drawing was finished in April 1501, they placed it on display. For two days, the people of Florence filed through the room and lingered before the drawing, "stupefied," wrote one observer, "by its perfection."

As Isabella d'Este was well aware, a drawing does not a painting make, and Leonardo would spend years turning his cartoon of *The Virgin and Child with Saint Anne* into a painting, and even then it was never quite finished. Distracted by his need to secure a steady patron and further sidetracked by his obsession with geometry, he seemed helpless before his *impiacentissimo del pennello,* his "weariness of the paintbrush."

His solution, in such circumstances, was to pack up his brushes and leave. Accordingly, when the opportunity came in the summer of 1502 to work as a military engineer—the very post that had been denied him once by Duke Ludovico and again by the Venetian government—he found himself bidding good-bye to the good monks of the Annunziata.

For all the attraction of his new job, Leonardo did not accept it without misgivings. Even as he made his way to the town of Faenza in the Papal States, where he was to meet his new employer, he continued to mull over what he was about to become and what he might now have to do in the name of the ruthlessly ambitious Cesare Borgia. But on a day like this, so warm, with sunlight etching every last olive tree against a robin's-egg sky, it was easy to forget that Italy was again a battleground and that this time it was the pope himself, Alexander VI, the father of Cesare Borgia, who was responsible. As for Cesare himself, Leonardo had heard enough about him to be wary—enough that he could agree with the commentator who had recently said of all the Borgias, "These people thirst for human blood."

All that talk—of the stabbings, the poisonings, the drownings—troubled him, as it should trouble anyone, Leonardo thought. And how could he, a vegetarian who would not make his own body "a tomb for other animals," reconcile his own beliefs with his willingness to work for such a man as Cesare Borgia? Was it just ambition—or some greater weakness; or was it the same quiet detachment that led him to devise a method whereby he could dissect the dead without ever dirtying his fingernails? Would he be able to do Borgia's bidding in the same detached manner? He could only try, he told himself, and if worse did come from this worst of human beings, leave.

To Borgia, Leonardo was, in the words of the passport issued in the latter's name, "our most excellent and well-beloved serv-

AL · DVS ·

AN ABUNDANCE OF BOOKS

Printing transformed the world during the Renaissance by facilitating learning and communication. Italy led the field with 73 presses, one of which was run by Aldus Manutius, who published most of the major classics of antiquity in high-quality editions. His Aldine Press in Venice adopted as its logo a dolphin weighed down by an anchor *(left),* which is an emblem of the motto "Hasten slowly."

In 1501 the press published a volume of Virgil's poetry *(below).* It was the first in a series of pocket-size books printed in a new typeface called italic. These stylish *libri portatiles,* or "portable books," sold well to educated merchants and nobles like Isabella d'Este, who probably owned this copy.

ALDVS STVDIOSIS OMNIBVS. S.

P·V·M·Bucolica·Georgica·Aeneida quam emendata, et qua forma damus, uidetis, cætera, quæ Poeta exercēdi sui gratia composuit, et obscœna, quæ eidem adscribuntur, nō cēsuimus digna enchiridio. Est animus dare posthac iisdem formulis optimos quosque autores.   Valete.

IN GRAMMATOGLYPTAE LAVDEM.

Qui graiis dedit Aldus, en latinis Dat nunc grammata sculpta dædaleis Francisci manibus Bononiensis.

P·V·M·MANTVANIBV COLICORVM TITYRVS.

Melibœus · Tityrus·

ityre tu patulæ recubās sub tegmine fagi   Me.
Syluestrem tenui musam meditaris auena.
Nos patriæ fines, et dulcia linquimus arua,
Nos patriam fugimus, tu Tityre lentus in mbra
Formosam resonare doces Amaryllida syluas.
O Melibœe, deus nobis hæc ocia fecit.   Ti.
Nanq; erit ille mihi semper deus. illius aram
Sæpe tener nostris ab ouilibus imbuet agnus.
Ille meas errare boues, ut cernis, et ipsum
Ludere, quæ uellem, cælamo permisit agresti.
Non equidem inuideo, miror magis. undiq; totis Me.
Vsque adeo turbatur agris. en ipse capellas
Protinus æger ago. hanc etiam uix Tityre duco.
Hic inter densas corylos modo nanq; gemellos,
Spem gregis, ah silice in nuda connixa reliquit.
Sæpe malum hoc nobis, si mens non leua fuisset,
De cœlo tactas memini prædicere quercus.
Sæpe sinistra caua prædixit ab ilice cornix.
Sed tamen, iste deus qui sit, da Tityre nobis.
Vrbem, quam dicunt Romam, Melibœe putaui Ti.
Stultus ego huic nostræ similem. quo sæpe solemus

ant, architect and engineer in chief." And with the freedom this passport promised him, Leonardo now roamed the countryside, taking the lay of the land and drawing up maps that Borgia could use in his various offensives. A number of towns were fortified on the engineer in chief's instructions, plans were made to construct a canal that would give the town of Cesena easier access to its harbor, and Leonardo further busied himself with a scheme for draining the pestilential marshes along the Tuscan coast.

It struck Leonardo as fitting that so much of his time should be occupied with the taming of water. For as long as he could remember he had been fascinated by water: its very fluidity, its inherent violence, its grace and potential. And almost without being aware of it, he would take up a piece of chalk or a pencil and begin forming eddying breakers or tracing long, languorous curves along a sheet of paper. Maybe a bridge would appear or the latest version of the mill he dreamed of building; or perhaps an entire town would dissolve in a wall of water, with the artist playing God to his own Deluge. "Ah, what dreadful tumults one heard resounding through the gloomy air!" Leonardo scribbled alongside one such drawing. "Ah me, how many lamentations!"

Had Leonardo chosen to listen, lamentations might have been heard throughout central Italy, as Cesare Borgia continued his northward advance, laying siege to town after town and summarily dealing with any who dared to threaten his progress. But the artist, who disdained sleep as the mimic of death, appears not to have lost much over his employer's excesses. Only when Borgia had two of his lieutenants—both foolish enough to lead a rebellion against their leader, and one a friend of Leonardo's—lured into a trap and strangled on the spot, did the engineer in chief resign his post and hurry back to Florence.

Florence's spindled skyline never looked as good to Leonardo da Vinci as it did on that spring day in 1503 when he caught his first glimpse of the city upon his return from the south. Still, it was an aimless Leonardo who had come home, with all of his acknowledged promise but with no immediate prospects of work.

Mindful, at the age of 51, that "nothing flows faster than the years," Leonardo managed to keep himself busy for several months by sharing his military expertise with the Florentine authorities. By October, though, the intervention of his friend Niccolò Machiavelli, now chancellor of the Florentine government, whom Leonardo had met during his tenure with Borgia, ensured a return to gentler pursuits. With an advance to purchase supplies, and an apartment and workshop to sweeten the deal, he was commissioned to paint a mural on one wall of the Grand Council Chambers, then under construction in the Palazzo della Signoria.

Military life had done nothing to increase Leonardo's efficiency, however, and true to form, a year later he was only getting around to setting up scaffolding and arranging and rearranging the tables that would hold his pots of paints. But by then he was no longer the only artist working in the low, dark hall, since the city's fathers had decided that the opposite wall needed a mural as well. They had also selected the man to paint it: the 29-year-old Michelangelo Buonarroti.

The two artists needed no introduction. Each was aware of the other's reputation, and their esteem for their respective talents was genuine. At the same time, an aging Leonardo didn't need reminding that he had little to show for his recent efforts; the painting for the Annunziata altar was still far from complete and the portrait of Isabella d'Este not even begun. The brash, young Michelangelo, on the other hand, was fresh from a pair of successes, having completed the *Pietà* in Rome to great acclaim, then, after his return to Florence in 1501, winning more fame for his statue of David.

For his part, Michelangelo was glad to be back in Florence. Rome under the Borgias was a city that had "closed the way to every goodness," a place where it might have been difficult to sort the murderers and thieves of the streets from those who lurked in the Vatican, were it not for the clerical robes worn by the latter. Yet, as he discovered upon his arrival, Florence, though eminently safer, was not the city he had left five years earlier.

To be sure, the city itself was unchanged. There were the same slender houses, top-heavy with balconies that shaded the narrow streets; the same bottegas, their awnings like eyelids over the doorways; the familiar Mercato Vecchio, where the smells rising from the butchers' stalls still vied with those wafting from the fishmongers' booths; and fronting on the wide Via Larga, the Palazzo Medici, as imposing now as it had been when it was first built half a century earlier.

But while it might be the same city he had grown up in, too many of the people Michelangelo had grown up with were gone: his old master, Domenico Ghirlandaio, for example, so generous of his time and talent, the man who had taken the 13-year-old Michelangelo on as an apprentice over the objections of the boy's father, dead even before his more famous pupil had left for Rome; and Lorenzo de' Medici—Il Magnifico himself—who had chosen Michelangelo as one of two apprentices to live and study in his palace, gone too these many years.

And of those the artist had met while

Leon Battista Alberti's facade for Santa Maria Novella in Florence features a two-tone color scheme defining its underlying geometric order, a signature of Renaissance style.

A REVOLUTION IN ART

During the Renaissance, Italian art underwent an extraordinary revolution. Although the era's architects, painters, and sculptors sought to revive classical motifs, they did not merely mimic the works of ancient Rome. Instead, they adapted the classical vocabulary to a new language of style that was inspired as much by humanism as by the techniques and styles of antiquity. At the heart of humanist philosophy was the belief that man is the measure of all things, and that concept shone through in Renaissance art.

Architects of the Renaissance expressed their humanistic beliefs by focusing on the individual viewer's experience. Worshipers in churches built by these architects felt God serenely surrounding them rather than soaring above them, as in Gothic buildings. The design emphasized harmony and clarity, with simple proportions relating each part of a building to the whole as well as the scale of the building itself to the human observer.

The Renaissance style of architecture owed much to one man: Filippo Brunelleschi, a Florentine goldsmith and sculptor by training and the designer of the dome of Florence's cathedral. Brunelleschi was among the first artists to study and measure ancient Roman buildings. He fused their classical features with mathematically based designs to create a style that paid

The 16th-century architect Andrea Palladio designed palaces and villas as well as churches. His Villa Rotonda, near Vicenza *(above)*, suggests the Pantheon merged with a freestanding round temple.

Inside Santo Spirito, a Florentine church begun in the 1430s, the architect Filippo Brunelleschi used classical columns, capitals, and architraves to draw one's eye toward the altar, the focal point of his design.

135

homage to antiquity but had an elegant simplicity that was entirely novel. Later architects of the Renaissance such as Leon Battista Alberti and Andrea Palladio followed Brunelleschi's lead.

Renaissance painters also strove to portray the divine beauty that existed on earth. Taking their cue from early-14th-century painter Giotto, renowned for his realistic style, artists began to depict humans and the world as naturally as possible. In their quest for realism, painters studied both classical sculpture and human anatomy. They tried in their work to follow Alberti's advice: "Begin with the bones. Then add the muscles, and then cover the body with flesh in such a way as to leave the position of the muscles visible." To master the illusion of space, they perfected two critical techniques: linear perspective and foreshortening. Artists utilized linear perspective to represent receding space on a flat surface and foreshortening to give objects a three-dimensional look.

As painters refined these techniques, they became less obsessed with anatomical correctness and with what the artist Paolo Uccello reportedly called his "sweet mistress," perspective. Later artists felt free to explore man's—and woman's—interior beauty. The paintings of Sandro Botticelli, for example, celebrated the sensuality of the nude, while Leonardo da Vinci, in his portraits, sought to reveal his subject's inner life.

In this 1425 painting, *Holy Trinity*, Masaccio demonstrates a stunning mastery of linear perspective. The barrel vault is perfectly rendered mathematically, and the figures placed inside and outside the chapel enhance the sense of receding space.

Sandro Botticelli's *Birth of Venus*, painted around 1482, illustrates two trends in Renaissance painting: veneration of ideal beauty and a growing interest in nonreligious subjects, especially those from classical mythology.

In a presentation typical of Renaissance portraiture, the sitter in Leonardo da Vinci's *Mona Lisa* faces the viewer so as to reveal, in his own words, "the motions of the mind."

he was a member of Lorenzo's household, who was left? Not the humanists Giovanni Pico della Mirandola and Marsilio Ficino, nor the poet Poliziano, nor the artist Antonio Pollaiuolo, whom Lorenzo had once dubbed "the greatest master in the city." All those who had enlivened the dinner conversations at the Palazzo Medici and who had introduced the receptive Michelangelo to classical philosophy and filled his head with all manner of ideas, not the least of them the humanist notion that one's physical form mirrors the state of his soul, all of them were gone.

Except for the loss of his mother, who had died when he was just a boy, Michelangelo's own family was largely intact. His bureaucrat father, who had resisted Michelangelo's desire to become an artist because he viewed craftsmen as social inferiors, was still his headstrong self, supporting the artist's four brothers.

It seemed, however, that the father would never accept his son's choice of career. Even the success of the *Pietà,* a triumph for any sculptor, let alone one so young, had failed to move the older Buonarroti. To the contrary, Lodovico Buonarroti could not for the life of him understand how his son had managed to win so much fame but so little fortune. "A glorified stonemason, that's all he is," the father would declare; "my own son, a glorified stonemason."

That his father was himself a mere clerk in the custom house was beside the point. All that mattered to Lodovico was that the Buonarrotis were of good stock, of noble stock even, and entitled to better than they were getting these days.

His father's pride, misplaced as it might have been, did have an effect on the son's determination to restore his family's good name. Indeed, the memories of his years in Rome were too recent for Michelangelo to forget how he had lived there on so little. He needed no reminding, too, that his own abstemious lifestyle—sleeping four to a bed to save money, making do with a crust of bread, working and sleeping in the same dirty clothes—was what allowed him to send money home for the support of his father and brothers and, later on, to purchase the real estate and make the business investments he hoped would buy his family its rightful place in Florentine society.

Money had, in fact, been much on Michelangelo's mind three years earlier, when

The man had botched his would-be Hercules and had lacked the skill to undo his own mistakes.

Secretive as always, Michelangelo had immediately ordered the block to be hidden from view behind a wooden enclosure. Meanwhile, he completed his models for the statue, so that within a month he was ready to begin work on the statue itself. Then, hour after hour, day after day, chisels rang on rock, as the sculptor, a summer of sweat staining his clothing, gave shape to the misshapen block, removing, as he was heard to say, "everything that was not David."

What emerged, to no one's surprise—at least not to anyone who knew Michelangelo—was a decidedly nude David, with no drapery to shield viewers from the statue's brazen indelicacy. The Giant, as Michelangelo liked to think of him, was as tall as the block of marble would allow, with huge hands and an outsize head. But as its sculptor stepped back for a last look, smearing a sweaty

"A glorified stonemason, that's all he is; my own son, a glorified stonemason."

he accepted the commission to sculpt what would become *David*. Equally enticing was the challenge to carve not just a figure, but a giant figure, large enough that when it was mounted on one of the cathedral's buttresses, observers on the ground would still be struck by the statue's grandeur. As if that weren't difficult enough, Michelangelo was to carve the figure from another sculptor's discarded block of marble.

His first look at the raw marble had not inspired confidence, Michelangelo remembered. Circling the 18-foot-high block, his brown eyes darting up and down, he had seen at once why Donatello's assistant had abandoned the piece some 40 years earlier:

paste of marble dust across his face with a dirty sleeve and pushing stray chips to one side with his foot, he looked up at a statue that was more than statue—a statement, a boast even, trumpeting a city's pride as much as his own daring and the shepherd David's courage. In its perfection, too, Michelangelo could see his own belief that the body was indeed the very mirror of the soul.

By the time *David* was finished in 1504, a committee of artists, architects, and citizens had decided that the statue should be placed in full view in front of the Palazzo della Signoria rather than atop one of the cathedral's buttresses, although full view to one of the committee's more prudish members, Leonardo da

The dead Christ of Michelangelo's *Pietà* lies cradled in Mary's lap, his limbs falling as gracefully as the folds of her gown. Images of the Pietà—the term for the crucified Christ in his mother's arms—usually were scenes of agony. But Michelangelo chose to ennoble his figures by using classical restraint. His *Pietà* was displayed in St. Peter's in 1500. After he overheard pilgrims attribute his work to someone else, Michelangelo carved his name on the band across the Virgin's chest.

Vinci, meant "with decent adornment." But moving the Giant was itself a gigantic proposition that took four days, with the statue slung in a sling suspended from a wooden frame and eased along greased beams by 40 men. A worried Michelangelo watched the statue's wobbly progress through the pinched streets, his anxiety sharpened by an attack of vandalism before the move had even begun. Several vandals, perhaps offended by the statue's nudity or maybe by its political symbolism, had hurled stones at the monument under cover of darkness. Afterward, a guard had to be posted to prevent further incidents.

With a brass garland affixed to the front of the statue for modesty's sake, *David* had only begun to attract crowds to the Piazza della Signoria when Michelangelo found himself sharing space with Leonardo in the Grand Council Chambers, the former sketching his plan for *The Battle of Cascina,* the latter preparing to paint his version of *The Battle of Anghiari.*

By then, each man had reason to be rankled by the presence of the other, Michelangelo having insulted the older artist with a rash comment about the latter's unfinished bronze horse for the duke of Milan, and Leonardo having offended his younger colleague by insisting that *David*'s nudity be less blatant. The two men had their philosophical differences as well, with the deeply religious Michelangelo matching the faith Leonardo put in science and nature with his own devotion to God and to art for art's sake. Moreover, the fastidious Leonardo had only to glance up from his work in the council chambers to see the burly, slightly hunchbacked, altogether graceless Michelangelo and to curl his lip in disgust: the filthy clothes, the younger man's unwashed body, the quick tongue, even his broken nose, earned—and no doubt deserved—years ago in a fistfight with the sculptor Pietro Torrigiano.

Fortunately for both men, they were not long in one another's company. Early in 1505 Michelangelo was summoned to

Rome by Pope Julius II, who, with an eye to eternity, desired a tomb suited to his station.

As with his statue of David, the challenge was irresistible and the pay substantial. Michelangelo quickly generated several designs, one of which, encompassing dozens of statues and several bronze reliefs in a three-story-high edifice, was approved by the pontiff. By April, undaunted by the task he had cut out for himself, Michelangelo was on his way to the quarries at Carrara, there to handpick each marble block that would be used for the tomb.

In the quarries Michelangelo was a happy man. Everywhere he looked he could envision statues hewn from individual blocks, monuments from uncut columns, whole colossi carved from entire cliffs. Running a callused hand across one rough slab, he imagined he could feel what the rock wanted to be. "There is nothing the greatest artist can conceive," he mused, "that every marble block does not confine within itself."

What he could not envision was that he would spend the better part of a year at Carrara choosing and personally supervising the cutting of each stone. Ton by wearying ton, the stones were sliced free from the mountain and eased down the slopes, every step freighted with the threat of sudden death, the workers stripped to their waists in the heat of the unblinking sun. The quarried stones were then floated on boats down the coast to Rome and trundled to St. Peter's, the marble filling half the piazza in front of the basilica.

The sight of all that marble gleaming in the square made Michelangelo eager to begin work. Bad weather had in fact delayed the arrival of the stone, but he had not wasted a moment, having already turned a house near St. Peter's into a workshop and a dormitory for himself and his assistants. Pope Julius, too, was anxious for work to get under way and, much to the solitary Michelangelo's dismay, had a mobile footbridge installed to allow easy access to the workshop from the Vatican.

But the pope was less available when it came to money. By April 1506, having tried patience and a few tactful hints, an exasperated Michelangelo had no choice but to confront the Holy Father. Respectful, but showing none of the submissiveness due a patron—let alone a pope—the sculptor pressed the issue. He went to see the pontiff and, looking Julius firmly in the eye, demanded payment.

At this, several of the pope's retinue pointedly cleared their throats, their satin robes swishing, eyes flicking in the direction of this upstart of a stonemason. Ignoring what another might have taken as an insult, His Holiness begged Michelangelo to return on the other side of Easter, two days later.

On Easter Monday, Michelangelo was back, only to be turned away. He returned the following day and every day thereafter, until finally on Friday he was, in his words, "sent packing." His steps sped by his hair-trigger temper, Michelangelo raced back to his workshop and furiously pounded from room to room scooping up his belongings in his muscled arms. Without a word to his employer, he was gone, his course set for Florence.

Had he overreacted? Back in Florence, Michelangelo still couldn't be certain. In any case, he would not be bullied, not even by the pope. Responding to a letter from Rome's pub-

With his craggy features and flattened nose, Michelangelo considered himself unattractive. But as this bust by Daniele da Volterra shows, he was a commanding presence, a man with an appearance of enormous physical strength and single-minded intensity.

lic works director, he allowed that he was entirely willing to complete the tomb—but in his studio in Florence, not in Rome. "So if His Holiness wishes to proceed," he declared, "let him make me over the deposit here in Florence, and I'll write to tell him where to send it."

For an artist to make such demands of the pope signaled a new level of effrontery, sparking a barrage of letters from Rome and return salvos from Florence. By summer's end, with the stakes mounting, the Signoria of Florence finally intervened in the matter. "You've tried and tested the pope as not even the king of France would dare," the gonfalonier of justice, Piero Soderini, told Michelangelo. "We don't want to wage war with him over you and put our state at risk."

Unswayed, Michelangelo bided his time, even as Pope Julius was himself preoccupied with a military campaign against Bologna. But in November word came that the pontiff, suddenly conciliatory, wished to see his bullheaded sculptor in Bologna, hinting that a different commission might be in the offing. A few weeks later, standing across from the seated pope, the 31-year-old Michelangelo dared to have the last word. Asked by Julius why he had hurried from Rome and left his work undone, the sculptor honed his words like a favorite chisel. "Not from ill will," he said, before applying the edge, "but from disdain."

With uncharacteristic forbearance, Pope Julius rewarded Michelangelo for his insolence with a commission to cast a bronze likeness of himself. Almost immediately, the sculptor came to understand that while he may have been forgiven, he had also been given a penance that would consume the next year of his life. Nor was his atonement at an end, as the pope made clear in 1508, when Julius summoned Michelangelo to Rome for a new assignment.

Offered the opportunity to paint the ceiling of the Sistine Chapel, Michelangelo at first wanted no part of it. "The place is

THREE RENAISSANCE WOMEN

The lot of most women in Renaissance Italy was much as it had been in the Middle Ages. They toiled at home or in the fields and took care of their families. They were expected to be modest and retiring and to appear only rarely in public. And in all things they were to defer to the will of their husbands, who, as one famous 15th-century preacher noted, had the right to use violence on them. "I say to you men," declared Saint Bernardino of Siena, "never beat your wives while they are great with child, for therein would lie great peril. I say not that you should never beat them; but choose your time."

Except for those who entered religious orders, only the very rich could escape such a life. Freed by wealth from the usual female responsibilities, upper-class women could rise above the bondage of their medieval past. It was sometimes possible for them to assume new roles and to act on their own desires and inclinations. Wealthy women could express their independence by patronizing the arts or other causes, by becoming scholars, or by developing their own talents and skills.

Still, these women faced an uphill battle for acceptance and recognition from men, while those who lacked the benefits of wealth or education continued their age-old struggle to survive and nurture their loved ones. But in the ripe setting of the Renaissance, the beginnings of modern woman were taking root. Depicted at right are three Renaissance women who made their own way in the world: Caterina Sforza, Vittoria Colonna, and Sofonisba Anguissola—warrior, poet, and painter, respectively.

VITORIA COLVMNA

With great courage and ingenuity, Caterina Sforza *(above)* defended her city, Forlì, against the forces of Cesare Borgia. She was captured, imprisoned, and possibly, raped by Borgia. But in the end she triumphed: She outlived Borgia, and in 1537 her grandson became the first duke of Florence.

Poet Vittoria Colonna came under the surveillance of the Inquisition for being sympathetic to the Reformation. Well known in her time, she also drew the attention of Michelangelo, who referred to her as his "untouched goddess."

Sofonisba Anguissola was one of the first famous women painters. After starting with relatives' portraits, she obtained commissions from afar and spent time at the Spanish court of Philip II, teaching the queen to paint.

143

wrong," he told the pontiff in his usual matter-of-fact manner, "and no painter am I." Others were more skilled with the brush, he argued, while his own love had always been for stone. And what of His Holiness's tomb? Wasn't it to be finished?

But this time the pope would hear no arguments. The Sistine Chapel was to be painted, and Michelangelo was to paint it. The artist, Julius commanded, was to start immediately; the tomb could wait.

Asked later in life why he had never married, Michelangelo explained, "I have only too much of a wife in my art, and she has given me trouble enough." One look at the ceiling in the Sistine Chapel would have any observer concurring with him. For starters, it was 80 feet high—he would need scaffolding, and even then would have to lie on his back or stand with his neck craned backward. Worse, the scaffolding could not be supported from the floor, since the chapel had to remain in use. And Michelangelo would have to work in fresco, with only hours in which to apply the colors while the plaster was still wet. It was hot in there, too, and dusty and dark; he would need torches, lots of torches, even in daylight.

Nor did it help that the pope had left the subject matter up to the artist. Not only would Michelangelo have to struggle with technique, but with no program, he would have to wrestle with theme, composition, form, even with an underlying philosophy. Years, he thought to himself with resignation, this was going to take him years.

Working with his usual speed, Michelangelo laid out a plan that met with the pope's approval. He would depict the Creation and Fall, as well as the drunkenness of Noah and other scenes from the Old Testament. Throughout the latter half of 1508, the work went smoothly enough: The scaffolding was in place by July; assistants were hired, and some just as quickly fired, Michelangelo in his impatience not tolerating even the slightest incompetence; sketches became cartoons, and the outlines of

these were incised onto the arriccio, the basecoat of plaster.

With the start of the new year, Michelangelo could daily be found high in the scaffolding, often as not standing on tiptoe, his right hand ending in a brush, its tip to the ceiling. "Bow-like," he wrote of the work, "I strain towards the skies." Though straining, he worked quickly, the fresh plaster almost immediately wet with paint, the latter applied in thin, transparent layers. Yet, the physical effort was so excruciating that he could be forgiven his perennial shortness of temper: "I live in hell and paint its pictures."

The ceiling was consuming Michelangelo's life. "I have no friends of any sort and want none," he lamented to one of his brothers in 1509. "I do not even have time to eat properly." Hardly a day passed that the painting didn't present a new problem, either of technique or of composition, at times forcing work to a stop until the artist could devise a solution. And there was no one else to turn to: His assistants were useless—the brushwork was almost entirely his own. The ceiling had come to dominate his thoughts even as it filled the hours of his days and, frequently, his nights. Too often sleepless, Michelangelo could be seen haunting the scaffolding in the dead of night, ribbons of smoke curling from a candle in his cap, his shadow swirling wildly across the ceiling.

To make matters worse, Michelangelo was again frustrated by the pope's forgetfulness when payments came due. Nor was his family of any comfort: His father was constantly in need of money, even on one occasion dipping into the artist's bank account without permission. One brother, the most shiftless of the lot, caused Michelangelo to threaten him with physical harm, and another, the artist's favorite, at one point was deathly ill. "I live with the greatest toil and a thousand worries," he would confess to his father before the ceiling was finished. "It has now been about 15 years since I have had a happy hour."

Only in the act of painting could Michelangelo lose himself,

Standing 14 feet tall, Michelangelo's colossal *David* appears invincible. Yet the face of the biblical hero is full of apprehension as he contemplates hurling his stone at Goliath. For the Florentines, David was a symbol of their strength and freedom.

Michelangelo's Sistine Chapel ceiling, unveiled in 1512, chronicles biblical history from the Creation to the Great Flood, with Old Testament prophets and pagan sibyls on thrones around the sides. The monumental scale and dynamic composition of the masterpiece, together with its brilliant use of color and perspective and the humanity of its godly figures, engendered a new order of expressive power.

Ironically, Michelangelo felt painting was not his strong point, and he painted the ceiling under duress. He preferred to sculpt, and frescoing the enormous vault was grueling. Yet the artist dared not defy the imperious Pope Julius II. In the sonnet below, Michelangelo vented his displeasure, adding a wry sketch of himself at work.

I've got myself a goiter from this strain,
As water gives the cats in Lombardy
Or maybe it is some other country;
My belly's pushed by force beneath my chin.

My beard toward Heaven, I feel the back of my brain
Upon my neck, I grow the breast of a Harpy;
My brush, above my face continually,
Makes it a splendid floor by dripping down.

My loins have penetrated to my paunch,
My rump's a crupper, as a counterweight,
And pointless the unseeing steps I go.

In front of me my skin is being stretched
While it folds up behind and forms a knot,
And I am bending like a Syrian bow.

147

and only the painting itself gave him pleasure. Here were God and Adam, almost fingertip to fingertip; God dividing light from darkness; Eve tempted in the garden; Noah stupefied by drink—every panel infused with the weight of fate, the glow of faith, the soul's relentless quest for the light of salvation, that endless struggle conveyed in writhing bodies and contorted faces. Alone on the scaffolding, Michelangelo was alone in the world, his own God in a world of his own making.

The ceiling was only half-finished in 1510 when Pope Julius, much to Michelangelo's annoyance, threw open the doors to the public. At the same time he ordered the sculptor to speed things up. "It is our pleasure," announced the pope, "that you should satisfy us in our desire to have it done quickly," adding that if Michel-

the ceiling of the Sistine Chapel, Michelangelo, his face showing both exhaustion and exhilaration, watched as the last of the scaffolding was dismantled. He was there again the next day, when Pope Julius entered the chapel in a phalanx of Vatican courtiers. Eyes to heaven, the pope spun slowly in a small circle, absorbing, with smug satisfaction, what the hand of one man had wrought. It was magnificent, he hardly had to tell Michelangelo, but might be made more so, he thought, with the slightest embellishment. "It must still be necessary to have it retouched with gold," the pontiff ventured, his eyes meeting Michelangelo's and reading disbelief.

The people of Rome saw no need for improvement, however. Crowding into the chapel, they gazed upward, "speechless with astonishment." What they saw were scenes that were famil-

"I live in hell and paint its pictures."

angelo refused, His Holiness would see to it that the artist was hurled from the scaffolding.

Thumping around on the quaking platform, a brush in one hand and a fistful more in the other, Michelangelo worked now like a man possessed. His face and beard constantly stippled with paint, he labored in a kind of disembodied frenzy that would move a later pope to comment on the *terribilità* of the temperamental artist, the passionate fury that fueled his genius. "I toil harder than any man who ever was," Michelangelo wrote to one brother in July 1512, "unwell and with enormous effort; and yet I have the patience to reach the desired end."

The desired end was not much longer in coming. On All Saints' Day 1512, some four years after he had first climbed to

iar to them from the pages of the Bible, rendered in a manner that was at once awe inspiring and disturbing. What they didn't see was that in Michelangelo's own difficult climb to the height of the ceiling, the Renaissance, too, had reached its apogee. And the earlier optimism of the Renaissance had been darkened by Michelangelo's haunting reminder of humanity's inevitable destiny. As if to underscore that change, before the week was out, Michelangelo's friend Niccolò Machiavelli was himself suddenly out of a job, his fall from grace providing him with the opportunity to imagine his masterpiece, *The Prince,* with its evocation of humanity's inherent evil and its anointing of Cesare Borgia, the dark prince of the Renaissance, as "a model for all those who rise in power."

THE GLORY OF RENAISSANCE ARCHITECTURE

"Thou art Peter and upon this rock I will build my church," proclaims the Latin inscription that surrounds the interior dome of St. Peter's basilica in Rome. While this famous biblical passage is meant to support the concept of papal sovereignty, it also applies to the magnificent structure itself, a symbol of the church's stability and longevity. The construction of this monument to both the faith and the worldliness of the Renaissance church consumed a daunting 160 years, the reigns of 22 popes, and the contributions and collaborations of some of the 16th and 17th centuries' greatest artistic talents.

The basilica that stands today, however, is not the original St. Peter's. The emperor Constantine, the first Roman ruler to sanction Christianity, erected the old St. Peter's in the fourth century AD atop what is believed to be the apostle's grave. This earlier basilica was a splendid edifice, fronted by a spacious atrium and richly adorned with gold mosaics. But centuries of plunder by Rome's invaders, coupled with neglect during the century the papacy ruled from Avignon, took their toll on the building, and by the mid-1300s, the altar lamps had gone out and cattle grazed in the atrium. When the papal

schism ended and the pope returned to Rome in 1417, it was obvious that something had to be done to save the revered sanctuary.

Initially, plans called for the restoration of the old church. But when Julius II was elected pope in 1503, he launched an ambitious project to replace it with a totally new structure. To help finance this massive undertaking, Julius began offering papal indulgences—documents which promised forgiveness of sins *(left)*—as a reward to generous donors, and he appointed the noted architect Donato Bramante as project chief. Bramante, an admirer of the imperial Roman style, designed the church as a monumental square temple, with an interior shaped like a Greek cross; the structure was to be crowned by a gigantic dome. He then set about dismantling the old basilica, thus earning himself the sobriquet "master wrecker." But Julius's and Bramante's tenures were short lived—by 1514 both had died and the endeavor passed to Pope Leo X. He offered the project to his friend and protégé, Raphael. The new pontiff's coronation took place in a crowded tent that had been set up near the construction site. Although Rome boasted other spacious basilicas, it was incon-

The original basilica of St. Peter *(left),* reportedly built over the apostle's grave, fell into a state of ruin during the exile of the popes in Avignon, France.

Pope Julius II meets with three of St. Peter's principal architects in this painting by 18th-century French artist Horace Vernet: Michelangelo, at Julius's left; Bramante, showing Raphael's plan for the church; and Raphael, holding a sketch of one his Vatican Palace frescoes.

Donato Bramante's proposed basilica, with its twin towers, an enormous dome, and smaller cupolas, is represented on this bronze medal minted by Pope Julius II. Such medals may have been sold to raise money for the project. The pontiff, whose portrait graced the medal's obverse side, buried a dozen of the medals under the basilica's cornerstone on April 18, 1506, the day construction began.

ceivable that a pope might be crowned anywhere but next to the tomb of Saint Peter.

Over the next 32 years a succession of popes and their architectural protégés collaborated on the project. As chief architect, Raphael had added a nave to the central-plan structure, changing the basic design of the new basilica to a rectangular Latin cross. But he died before he could execute his plan and was succeeded in 1520 by Antonio da Sangallo, a colleague with whom he had worked amiably since 1516. Sangallo proposed several schemes and then devoted seven years to the construction of a huge wooden model of his intended masterpiece. While such models were the norm for Renaissance building projects, Sangallo's was deemed excessive because the price tag of the model alone equaled that of a fair-sized parish church, and the architect was further criticized for lining the pockets of his many relatives with funds earmarked for the basilica.

Little if any work had been done on the actual building since the death of Bramante. Construction had halted with only his four huge piers, intended to support the future dome, and the barrel vaults over the crossing arms towering over the remnants of the old basilica, while weeds flourished throughout the building site. But with Sangallo's death in 1546, the pace again picked up. The new chief architect who reluctantly accepted Pope Paul III's commission was the 71-year-old Michelangelo. The great master, who 34 years earlier had completed the arduous painting of the Vatican's Sistine Chapel, was tired and embittered and did not want

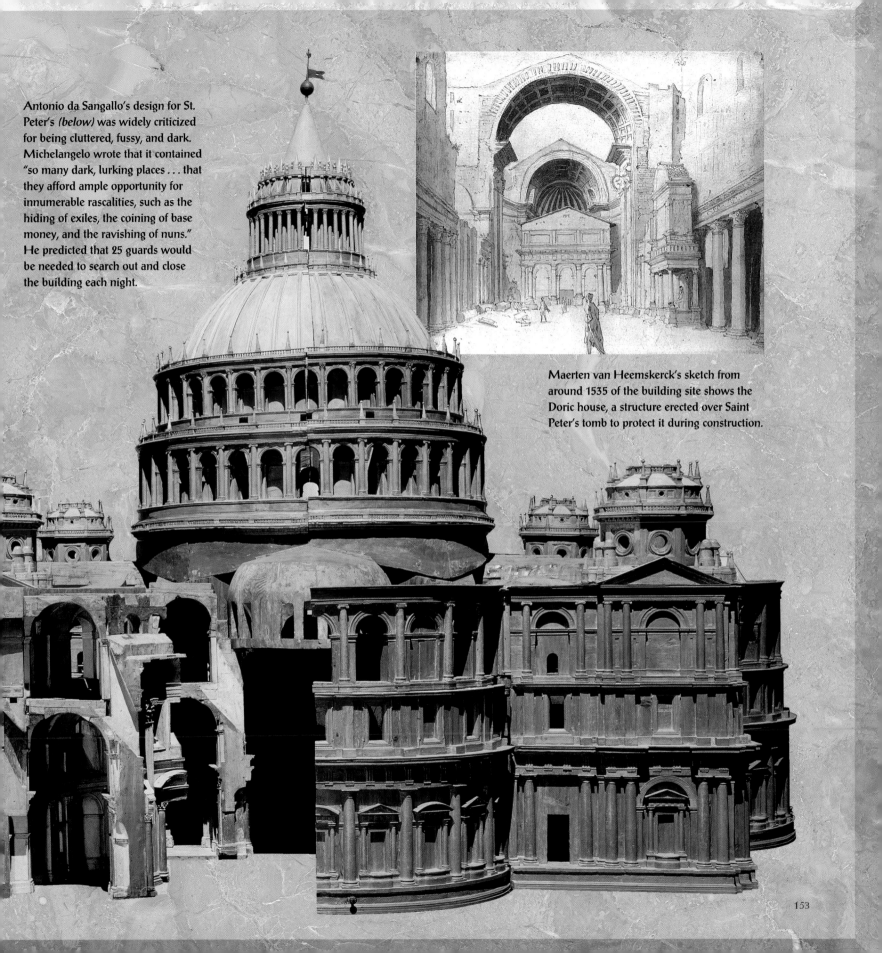

Antonio da Sangallo's design for St. Peter's *(below)* was widely criticized for being cluttered, fussy, and dark. Michelangelo wrote that it contained "so many dark, lurking places . . . that they afford ample opportunity for innumerable rascalities, such as the hiding of exiles, the coining of base money, and the ravishing of nuns." He predicted that 25 guards would be needed to search out and close the building each night.

Maerten van Heemskerck's sketch from around 1535 of the building site shows the Doric house, a structure erected over Saint Peter's tomb to protect it during construction.

153

Michelangelo, in black, presents a model of his proposed design to Pope Paul IV in a painting by Domenico Cresti da Passignano. The great master admired Brunelleschi's dome on Florence's cathedral and adopted its double-shell construction for St. Peter's.

This fresco from about 1590 depicts St. Peter's as Michelangelo might have envisioned it. Here, the building is rounder, the nave shorter, the dome slightly less elliptical, and the front projecting forward more than in the completed basilica.

A building stone is hoisted into St. Peter's partially built dome in this drawing by Giovanni Antonio Dosio made in 1564.

the job. "It was not of my willing that I built St. Peter's," he later wrote, but "for the glory of God, in honor of Saint Peter and for the salvation of my soul."

Michelangelo quickly scrapped most of Sangallo's designs, which he openly disparaged, and returned to Bramante's original concept for a central-plan church with a large dome. Building resumed, and over the following 17 years the basilica began to take shape, with the addition of the south apse, the foundations for two large chapels, and the drum of the dome. Then, in 1564, Michelangelo passed away, and again construction languished, this time for 24 years. Unlike his predecessors, however, Michelangelo had obtained written assurance from Pope Paul III that his design would prevail even after his death, and for the most part it did. In the late 1580s, Michelangelo's successor Giacomo della Porta and the renowned engineer Domenico Fontana finished the dome and portions of the interior, deviating only slightly from Michelangelo's plan.

However, another 36 years would pass before the building was completed, and by then the design would change yet again. The Counter Reformation had begun, and Pope Paul V wanted to emphasize the grandeur of Catholicism, and especially the papacy, with long ecclesiastical processions. He ordered architect Carlo Maderno, who was already working on the facade, to elongate the basilica's entrance arm by almost 200 feet to create a long nave. In complying, Maderno destroyed the sole surviving columns, walls, and priceless mosaics of the old St. Peter's.

On November 18, 1626, before a glittering throng of cardinals, ambassadors, and other dignitaries, Pope Urban VIII consecrated the new basilica. Its interior was still incomplete—the 40-year task of adorning it would fall primarily to the baroque architect Gianlorenzo Bernini, who would also design the elliptical colonnade leading to the church. But the major work was done, the monumental task finally finished, and the result would reign as the crowning glory of Renaissance architecture.

St. Peter's vast central nave, measuring more than 600 feet in length, was built by Carlo Maderno and decorated by baroque artists in the 17th century. The spectacular gilded bronze baldachin, or canopy, over the high altar was a masterpiece created by sculptor Gianlorenzo Bernini.

Despite minor changes to the exterior cupola, the 370-foot-high inner dome of St. Peter's was built to Michelangelo's exact specifications. Its magnificence inspired the 17th-century architect Carlo Fontana to declare it a "stupendous" work "never before equalled in the world," and to proclaim its creator a "great builder [who] will deserve to live eternally."

GLOSSARY

Antechamber: a small room serving as an entrance or service room for a larger, adjoining room.

Apostolic succession: the direct line of succession of Roman Catholic bishops from the apostles.

Apothecary: one who prescribes, mixes, and dispenses drugs and herbal remedies.

Apprentice: a boy or young man, usually bound by legal agreement, who works for a master in a guild in return for instruction in the guild's craft.

Apse: in architecture, a semicircular or polygonal, usually domed, projection of a church in which the altar is located.

Archipelago: a large body of water containing many islands; the group of islands scattered over such a body of water.

Architrave: in architecture, the lowest part of an entablature, resting directly on a column's capital.

Arriccio: in preparing a wall for a fresco, the first, coarser layer of plaster applied to the wall to which the outline of the painting is transferred.

Arsenal: name of the enormous complex of shipyards and associated workshops at Venice where ships, sails, ropes, and ordnance were made.

Ascetic: one who renounces material comforts and practices self-denial and austerity as either an act of personal discipline or religious devotion.

Astrology: a form of divination used to predict the destiny of individuals, groups, or nations, based on the theory that the stars, planets, sun, and moon have a direct influence on human affairs and natural earthly events.

Autocracy: a country or state ruled by one person, who has sole authority and unlimited power.

Babylonian exile: the period between 1309 and 1377 when the papal court left Rome for exile in Avignon, France; also called Babylonian captivity.

Backward script: a form of writing legible only in a mirror, used by Leonardo da Vinci in his notebooks; also called mirror writing.

Baldachin: in architecture, a freestanding, ornamental canopy consisting of four columns and a decorative roof, usually placed over an altar.

Baptistery: a part of a church or a separate, associated building used for baptisms.

Baroque: in art and architecture, a style that began in Italy in the latter half of the 16th century and spread through much of Europe, characterized in part by grandeur, richness, drama, vitality, and complexity of design.

Basilica: in Catholicism, a title of honor given to church buildings because of their antiquity or their role as international worship centers.

Billet: lodging for troops in tents or private homes.

Bottega: literally, "shop"; a studio-workshop serving as a studio and a factory, where an artist and assistants produced works of art as well as household and utilitarian objects.

Cabala: a system of mystical Jewish teachings.

Canon: a clergyman on the staff of a cathedral.

Canonic law: the body of law governing the faith and practice of the church and its members.

Capital: in architecture, the upper part of a pillar or column that provides support and which, in classical styles, is the most easily distinguishable feature in determining the type of column.

Carder: one who uses a wire-toothed brush, called a card, to cleanse and disentangle fibers, such as wool, prior to spinning.

Cartoon: a preliminary, full-size sketch of a subject to be used by the artist as a guide for producing a final painting, tapestry, mosaic, or fresco.

Cassone: an elaborately carved Italian chest, decorated with paintings and gilded; generally used as a marriage chest for a bride's dowry.

Chemise: a woman's loose undergarment, typically made of linen.

Ciao: literally, "I am your slave"; an expression of both greeting and farewell.

City-state: a sovereign state consisting of an independent city and the land and villages surrounding it, with the city serving as the political, economic, cultural, and social center of the area.

Colonnade: in architecture, a series of columns placed at regular intervals, often with a roof; used either independently as a walkway or as part of the building to which it is attached.

Column: in architecture, any vertical support consisting of a base, shaft, and capital, being at least four times as high as its diameter, with the shaft usually being circular or fluted.

Condottiere: a commander of a company of mercenaries.

Contrada: a district of a city or region.

Cornu: a close-fitting cap with a hornlike protrusion rising upward from the crown, worn by the doge of Venice.

Counter Reformation: a 16th- and early-17th-century reform movement in the Roman Catholic Church to counteract Protestantism.

Cuckold: a man whose wife is unfaithful to him.

Cuffia: a woman's cap embroidered with pearls and gold thread.

Cupola: in architecture, a domed interior ceiling; a small structure on a roof serving as a belfry or small dome.

Dialectics: the discipline of a formal logical argument in which several methods of arriving at the truth are used.

Doge: literally, "duke"; beginning in 697 and continuing until 1797, the chief magistrate and head of state of the republic of Venice, elected for life.

Double-entry bookkeeping: a method of record-keeping in which each financial transaction is entered as a debit to one account and as a credit to another so that debits and credits are always equal.

Doublet: a man's close-fitting, padded and waisted jacket, worn over a shirt and popular in Europe from the 15th to the 17th centuries.

Dowry: the money, goods, or estate brought by a bride to her husband upon marriage.

Dowry Fund: in Florence, the state-run dowry system in which parents could purchase shares for a daughter at her birth, redeemable with interest at her marriage.

Drum: in architecture, the circular or polygonal wall supporting a dome.

Duchy: the territory of a duke or duchess.

Epigram: a concise, witty poem expressing a single thought.

Excommunication: an ecclesiastical censure in which a person, city, or state is deprived of the rights of church membership, including the right to participate in the sacraments.

Facade: in architecture, a building's front or face.

Florin: a gold coin, first minted in Florence in 1252.

Foreshortening: the proportional shortening of the lines of an object in a drawing to create the illusion of its extension into space.

Foundling home: a home for orphans or abandoned infants of unknown parentage.

Fra: a title that precedes the name of an Italian monk or friar, generally equivalent to "brother."

Fresco: the art of painting on a fresh finishing coat of plaster before it dries, using pigments dissolved in water so that the painting becomes part of the wall; a painting executed in this manner.

Gonfalonier of justice: in Florence, the chairman of the Signoria, originally elected for a two-month term but by 1498 elected to the position for life.

Guilds: associations of craftsmen or merchants that organized, regulated, and restricted trade in products, crafts, or services and were active in the political and civic affairs of most medieval and Renaissance cities.

Humanism: a cultural and intellectual movement of the Renaissance that emphasized secular rather than religious studies and promoted the revival of interest in classical Greek and Roman writings, values, art forms, and philosophy.

Hydrodynamics: a branch of science pertaining to the motion of fluids and the forces acting on solid objects immersed therein.

Indulgence: the partial remission by the Roman Catholic Church of the punishment due for a sin that has been pardoned by performance of penance, granted by bishops, cardinals, and the pope.

Inquisition: an ecclesiastical tribunal established by the Roman Catholic Church in 1231 to pursue and punish those committing heresy and witchcraft, later extended to include those committing blasphemy and sacrilege as well.

Libri portatiles: literally, "portable books"; small, easily carried books first printed in 1501.

Linear perspective: an artistic technique in which parallel lines converge to give the illusion of depth and distance.

Lira: the basic monetary unit of Italy; the first coins were struck in the 16th century in several Italian city-states, and their value varied by weight until standardized in the mid-19th century.

Loggia: a roofed balcony, gallery, or porch, especially one on a second or higher story, overlooking an open court, the street, or a public square.

Lucco: a dark, ankle-length gown with buttons down the front, a hood like a monk's cowl, and full sleeves, worn, belted or unbelted, by virtually all Florentine men until the 1530s.

Lute: a stringed musical instrument with a large, pear-shaped body and a long neck, usually bent just below the tuning pegs, played by plucking the strings with the fingers and frequently used to accompany singers.

Madrigal: a vocal composition following a strict poetic form for two or more voices singing in simple harmony, with no accompaniment.

Maestro: literally, "master"; a guild artist or craftsman of great skill, qualified to establish his own workshop and practice independently and to teach the trade or craft to others.

Mercato Vecchio: the Old Market in Florence, the main shopping district of the city.

Mercenary: a professional soldier hired for service in a foreign army.

Nave: the central part of a church extending from the narthex (entrance hall) to the chancel (area behind the altar), usually flanked by aisles.

Neoplatonism: a philosophical system developed in the third century, based on Platonism but containing elements of mysticism and some Judaic and Christian concepts.

Nepotism: bestowing favors upon one's own relatives, particularly in business dealings or in employment.

Notary: in 15th-century Florence, a public official whose duties included supervising and attesting to the validity of wedding ceremonies.

Palazzo: a large, splendid private residence or public building; a palace.

Palio: literally, "banner"; an expensive gold-embroidered silk banner, sometimes trimmed in fur, given as the prize to the winner of any of the annual Italian horse races held on feast days; any of the horse races named after the prize.

Palle: literally, "balls"; on a coat of arms, round symbols representing the earth, coins, pills, fruit, or mythological events.

Pantomime: a form of entertainment, either a play or a dance, in which a story is told silently, through bodily movements, gestures, and facial expressions.

Papal Curia: the name given the papal bureaucracy in Rome that assists the pope in administering the affairs of the church.

Papal States: the areas in Italy and parts of France, varying in size over the centuries, that were ruled by the Roman Catholic Church from 754 until Italy was unified in 1870; today consisting only of Vatican City.

Patrimony: one's inheritance from one's father or other ancestor.

Patron: a benefactor; one who financially and morally encourages and supports an artist in his work or commissions.

Piazza: a public square in an Italian town, usually surrounded by buildings.

Platonic Academy: in mid-15th-century Florence, an informal group of humanists whose members met periodically to read from Plato's works and to study and debate his philosophy.

Podesta: the chief magistrate in Florence and many other medieval and Renaissance city-states.

Pontiff: the pope.

Popolo grasso: literally, "the well-fed people," or "the fat people"; generally, bankers, businessmen, doctors, and others of the wealthy middle class who dominated the economic and political life of a city-state.

Prelate: a high-ranking member of the clergy, especially a bishop.

Rack: an instrument of torture consisting of a large frame with rollers at either end to which the limbs were fastened and between which the body was stretched.

Reliquary: a small bag, casket, or other container in which sacred religious relics are kept or displayed.

Republic: a state in which the supreme power resides in a body of citizens entitled to vote; power is exercised by representatives chosen by the citizens.

Rialto: a marketplace; the commercial hub of the Venetian republic.

"Ring-day" ceremony: the wedding ceremony during which the bride and groom exchanged vows and a notary recorded their agreement to the union arranged by their fathers or male kin.

Sacristy: in a church, the room where the vestments and the sacred vessels are kept.

Savant: a learned person; a scholar.

Schema: a model, plan, or outline.

Scion: a descendant or an heir.

Shibboleth: a widely held belief.

Shot silk: silk with an iridescent quality, possessing changeable color effects or suffused with streaks of color.

Sobriquet: an affectionate, humorous, or descriptive nickname.

Soldi: prior to 1862, an Italian coin, 20 of which equaled one lira.

Sovereign state: any completely independent government having supreme power within its borders.

Spinoso: literally, "thorny," "spiny," or "prickly."

Stipend: a fixed sum of money paid regularly, either for services rendered or as an allowance.

Strappado: literally, "the rope"; a form of punishment or torture in which the victim's hands were tied behind his back and he was hoisted high and then dropped, so that his arms were almost torn from their sockets.

Studiolo: literally, "small study"; a small room or office in a Renaissance palace containing works of art, books, and objects of historic or scientific interest.

Sumptuary laws: laws designed to regulate the ownership and use of luxury goods, intended to restrict the finest possessions to those of the highest rank.

Sweetmeats: any sweet treat, particularly candies and candied fruit.

Tabernacle: the box on a Roman Catholic Church altar containing the consecrated elements of the Eucharist.

Tempera: a painting medium in which dry pigment is mixed with a water-soluble binder, such as egg yolk, and then thinned with water to the desired consistency.

Terra cotta: literally, "baked earth"; a glazed or unglazed fired clay used since ancient times for bricks, roof tiles, and pottery and, during the Renaissance, in sculpture and as a decorative building material.

Trompe l'oeil: literally, "fool the eye"; a style of painting in which objects are depicted so accurately that they appear to be real.

Underdress: a dress of wool or silk, worn beneath another, finer, dress, and sometimes designed with decorative portions intended to be displayed.

Vanities: objects deemed by the monk Savonarola likely to promote vanity or wickedness, such as mirrors and cosmetics or lascivious books and arts, which were seized and burned in a bonfire.

PRONUNCIATION GUIDE

Alamanno Salviati (ahl-ah-MAHN-oh)
Albizzi (ahl-BEET-tsee)
Aldus Manutius (AHL-duhs ma-NOO-shee-uhs)
Alfonso d'Este (ahl-FOHN-soh DEHST-ay)
Andrea Mantegna (ahn-DRAY-uh mahn-TEH-nyah)
Angelo Poliziano (AHN-jeh-loh poh-leet-see-YAH-noh)
Anghiari (ahn-ghee-AHR-ee)
Antonio Pollaiuolo (ahn-TOH-nee-oh pohl-lah-YWOH-loh)
Ariosto (ah-ree-OHS-toh)
Arriccio (ah-REE-chee-yoh)
Avignon (ah-vee-NYOHN)
Baldachin (BAHL-dah-kihn)
Baldassare Castiglione (bahl-dah-SAH-ray kah-stee-lee-YOH-nay)
Bartolommeo (bahr-toh-loh-MAY-oh)
Bergamo (BEHR-gah-moh)
Bernardo di Bandini Baroncelli (behr-NAHR-doh dee bahn-DEE-nee bah-rohn-CHEHL-lee)
Bessarion (bay-SAH-ree-ohn)
Boccaccio (boh-KAH-chee-oh)
Bologna (boh-LOH-nyuh)
Bottega (boh-TAY-guh)
Brescia (BRAY-shee-ah)
Bucintoro (byoo-cheen-TOH-roh)
Buonarroti (BWOHN-ah-ROH-tee)
Careggi (kah-REH-djee)
Carità (kah-ree-TAH)
Cascina (kah-SHEE-nuh)
Cassone (kahs-SOH-nay)
Cesare Borgia (CHEH-sah-ray BOR-jah)
Civettino (CHEE-veh-TEE-noh)
Collesalvetti (KOHL-leh-sahl-VEH-tee)
Colonna (koh-LOHN-nah)
Contrada (kohn-TRAH-duh)
Cuffia (KOO-fee-uh)
Dati (DAH-tee)
De Sphaera (deh SFAH-eh-ruh)
Doge (DOHJ)
Domenico Ghirlandaio (doh-MAY-nee-koh geer-lahn-DAH-yoh)
Donato Bramante (doh-NAH-toh brah-MAHN-tay)
Ercole (ehr-KOH-lay)
Ermolao Barbaro (EHR-muh-laoh BAHR-bah-roh)
Federigo (feh-deh-REE-goh)
Fiammetta Adimari (FEE-ah-MAY-tah ah-dee-MAHR-ee)
Filippo Brunelleschi (fee-LEE-poh broo-neh-LEHS-kee)
Forlì (fohr-LEE)
Francesco Granacci (frahn-CHAYS-koh grah-NAHT-chee)
Galeazzo (gah-lee-AHT-tsoh)
Gianfrancesco (jahn-frahn-CHAYS-koh)
Gianlorenzo (jahn-loh-REHN-zoh)
Girolamo Savonarola (GEE-roh-LAH-moh Sah-VOH-nah-ROH-lah)
Gonfalonier (gohn-fah-loh-NYEHR)
Gonzaga (gohn-ZAH-guh)
Gran cavallo (grahn kah-VAHL-loh)
Guarino da Verona (gwah-REE-noh dah veh-ROH-nah)
Guidobaldo da Montefeltro (gwee-doh-BAHL-doh dah mohn-teh-FEHL-troh)
Heraclitus (hayr-ah-KLEYE-tuhs)
Iacopo da Volterra (YAH-koh-poh dah vohl-TEHR-rah)
Il concetto dell' anima (eel kohn-CHEH-toh dehl AH-nee-mah)
Imola (EE-moh-lah)
Impiacentissimo del pennello (eem-pee-yuh-chehn-TEE-SEE-moh dehl PEHN-ehl-loh)
Isotta (ee-SOH-tah)
Libri portatiles (LEE-bree pohrt-tuh-TEE-lays)
Lodovico della Casa (loh-doh-VEE-koh deh-lah KAH-zah)
Loggia (LOH-djah)
Luca Pacioli (LOO-kuh pah-CHYOH-lee)
Lucco (LOO-koh)
Lucrezia (loo-KRAY-tsee-uh)
Ludovico Foscarini (loo-doh-VEE-koh fohs-kah-REE-nee)
Mandragola (mahn-DRAH-goh-lah)
Marsilio Ficino (mahr-SEE-lyoh fee-CHEE-noh)
Masaccio (mah-SAHT-chee-oh)
Massimiliano (MAHS-ee-mee-lee-YAH-noh)
Medici (MEH-dee-chee)
Mercato Vecchio (mehr-KAH-toh VEH-kee-yoh)
Michelozzo Michelozzi (mee-keh-LOHT-tsoh mee-keh-LOHT-tsee)
Modena (MOH-dehn-uh)
Nebbia (NEH-bee-uh)
Niccolò da Tolentino (nee-koh-LOH dah toh-lehn-TEE-noh)
Orsanmichele (ohr-SAHN-mee-KAY-lay)
Orseolo (ohr-say-OH-loh)
Ospedale degli Innocenti (OHS-pay-DAH-lay day-lee een-noh-CHEHN-tee)
Palazzo Davanzati (pah-LAHT-tzoh dah-vahn-ZAH-tee)
Palio (PAH-lee-oh)
Palle (PAHL-lay)
Passignano (pah-see-NYAH-noh)
Pazzi (PAHT-tsee)
Percussina (pehr-kuhs-SEE-nah)
Pesaro (PAY-sah-roh)
Piagnoni (pee-ah-NYOH-nee)
Pico della Mirandola (PEE-koh deh-lah mee-RAHN-doh-lah)
Piero di Cardinale (pee-AY-roh dee KAHR-dee-NAH-lay)
Piero Soderini (pee-AY-roh soh-deh-REE-nee)
Pietà (pee-ay-TAH)
Pietro Torrigiano (pee-AY-troh toh-ree-DJAH-noh)
Pinturicchio (peen-too-REE-kee-oh)
Pistoia (pee-STOY-ah)
Platina (plah-TEE-nah)
Podesta (poh-DEHS-tah)
Popolo grasso (POH-poh-loh GRAHS-soh)
Raffaele Riario (rahf-fah-YEHL-lay ree-AH-ree-oh)
Raphael (RAH-feye-ehl)
Reggio (REH-jee-oh)
Rialto (ree-AHL-toh)
Rinascimento (ree-nah-shee-MEHN-toh)
Romagna (roh-MAH-nyah)
Rovere (roh-VAY-ray)
Rovigo (roh-VEE-goh)
Rucellai (roo-cheh-LAH-ee)
Salai (sah-LAH-ee)
Salviati (sahl-vee-AH-tee)
San Frediano (sahn freh-dee-YAH-noh)
Sangallo (sahn-GAHL-loh)
Santissima Annunziata (sahn-TEES-see-mah ah-noon-tsee-AH-tah)
Septimius Severus (sep-TEE-mee-uhs suh-VEHR-uhs)
Sigismondo (see-jees-MOHN-doh)
Signoria (see-nyoh-REE-ah)
Sofonisba Anguissola (soh-foh-NEEZ-bah ahn-gwee-SOH-lah)
Soldi (SOHL-dee)
Spinoso (spee-NOH-soh)
Sposalizio del Mare (SPOH-sah-LEE-tzee-yoh dehl MAH-ray)
Strappado (strah-PAH-doh)
Studia humanitatis (STOO-dee-yah hoo-mah-nee-TAH-tees)
Studiolo (stoo-dee-YOH-loh)
Subiaco (soo-BYAH-koh)
Tornabuoni (tohr-nah-BWOH-nee)
Trieste (TREE-ehs-tay)
Urbino (oor-BEE-noh)
Verrocchio (vehr-ROHK-kee-oh)
Vespasiano da Bisticci (veh-SPAH-see-AHN-oh dah bee-STEE-chee)
Vicenza (vee-CHEHN-zah)
Vittorino da Feltre (vee-toh-REE-noh dah FEHL-tray)

ACKNOWLEDGMENTS AND PICTURE CREDITS

ACKNOWLEDGMENTS

The editors wish to thank the following individuals and institutions for their valuable assistance in the preparation of this volume:

Elisabeth Heinemann, Städelsches Kunstinstitut Frankfurt; Heidrun Klein, Bildarchiv Preussischer Kulturbesitz, Berlin; Marie Montembault, Département des Antiquités Grecques et Romaines, Musée du Louvre, Paris.

PICTURE CREDITS

The sources for the illustrations that appear in this volume are listed below. Credits from left to right are separated by semicolons, from top to bottom by dashes.

Cover: Erich Lessing Culture and Fine Arts Archives, Vienna/Uffizi, Florence.

1-5: Musei Vaticani, Rome. **6, 7:** Giancarlo Gasponi, Rome. **8-11:** Stefano Amantini/Schapowalow, Hamburg. **12, 13:** Maps by John Drummond, © Time Life Inc. **14, 15:** Scala, Florence. **16:** Erich Lessing Culture and Fine Arts Archives, Vienna/ Galleria delle Marche, Urbino, Italy; Erich Lessing Culture and Fine Arts Archives, Vienna/Palazzo Ducale, Urbino, Italy. **17:** Erich Lessing Culture and Fine Arts Archives, Vienna/Uffizi, Florence. **18:** Erich Lessing Culture and Fine Arts Archives, Vienna/Appartamento Borgia, Vatican City. **19:** Archiv für Kunst und Geschichte (AKG), Berlin; Scala, Florence. **20:** The Pierpont Morgan Library/Art Resource, N.Y.; Soprintendenza per i Beni Artistici e Storici di Modena, Galleria Estense, Modena. **21:** Biblioteca Estense Universitaria, Modena—Scala, Florence. **22, 23:** Alinari-Giraudon, Paris; Erich Lessing Culture and Fine Arts Archives, Vienna/ Louvre, Paris; Louvre, Paris/ET Archive, London; Biblioteca Estense Universitaria, Modena. **24:** Scala, Florence. **25:** Erich Lessing Culture and Fine Arts Archives, Vienna/Muzeum Narodowe Biblioteka Czartoryskich, Cracow, Poland; Scala, Florence. **26:** The Metropolitan Museum of Art, New York, gift of Henry G. Marquand, 1889. Marquand Collection (89.15.19). © 1992 The Metropolitan Museum of Art (detail). **27:** Copyright The British Museum, London. **28, 29:** Scala, Florence. **30:** Lauros-Giraudon, Paris. **31:** Page from *Aritmetica* by Filippo Calandri, woodcut, 1491, The Metropolitan Museum of Art, New York, Rodgers Fund, 1919. **33-35:** Border by John Drummond, © Time Life Inc. **33:** Scala, Florence. **34:** From *Tutto Su Firenze Rinascimentale* by Giunti Bemporad Marzocco, 1964, Flor-

ence—Scala, Florence. **35:** Scala, Florence—Erich Lessing Culture and Fine Arts Archives, Vienna/ Palazzo Davanzati, Florence. **36, 37:** Copyright National Gallery, London (attributed to Apollonio: Cassone with a Tournament Scene). **38, 39:** Private Collection/Bridgeman Art Library, London. **40:** Staatliche Museen zu Berlin-Preussischer Kulturbesitz, Gemäldegalerie, photo by Jörg P. Anders. **41:** Erich Lessing Culture and Fine Arts Archives, Vienna/Palazzo Davanzati, Florence. **43:** Rijksmuseum, Amsterdam. **44, 45:** Border by John Drummond, © Time Life Inc.—Scala/Art Resource, N.Y.—Scala, Florence; Erich Lessing Culture and Fine Arts Archives, Vienna/Ospedale del Ceppo, Pistoia, Italy—Scala/Art Resource, N.Y. **48:** Scala, Florence. **49:** From *Storia di Maria per Ravenna*. **50:** Artothek, Peissenberg/ Städelsches Kunstinstitut Frankfurt, photo by Ursula Edelmann. **53:** Mario Quattrone, Florence. **55:** Gianni Dagli Orti, Paris. **56:** Copyright The British Museum, London (2)—Scala, Florence. **58:** Giraudon, Paris. **59:** Kunsthistorisches Museum, Vienna. **61:** Scala/Art Resource, N.Y. **62, 63:** Artephot/Nimatallah (and background). **64, 65:** Erich Lessing Culture and Fine Arts Archives, Vienna/Museo Correr, Venice, Italy—courtesy Musée International de la Chaussure, Romans-sur-Isère; Scala, Florence (2, and background). **66, 67:** The British Library, London; copyright National Gallery, London (Italian Florentine School: *Portrait of a Lady in Red* [detail]); AKG, Berlin (and background); Scala, Florence. **68, 69:** Scala, Florence (and background); Witt Library, Courtauld Institute of Art, London. **69:** Scala, Florence (2). **70:** *Lorenzo de' Medici,* Samuel H. Kress Collection, © 1998 Board of Trustees, National Gallery of Art, Washington, D.C. **71:** Scala, Florence. **73:** Alinari, Florence; Scala/Art Resource, N.Y. **74, 75:** Scala, Florence. **77:** AKG, Berlin. **78:** *Giuliano de' Medici,* Samuel H. Kress Collection, © 1998 Board of Trustees, National Gallery of Art, Washington, D.C. **79:** Giraudon, Paris. **80:** Erich Lessing Culture and Fine Arts Archives, Vienna/Biblioteca Vaticana, Vatican City; Scala/Art Resource, N.Y. **81:** Scala/Art Resource, N.Y. (2); Ernst A. Heiniger. **82:** Erich Lessing Culture and Fine Arts Archives, Vienna/Biblioteca Vaticana, Vatican City; Erich Lessing Culture and Fine Arts Archives, Vienna/Uffizi, Florence—Biblioteca Apostolica Vaticana, Rome; Uffizi, Florence/ET Archive, London. **83:** Erich Lessing Culture and Fine Arts Archives, Vienna/ Biblioteca Vaticana, Vatican City. **84:** Scala, Florence. **86, 87:** Erich Lessing Culture and Fine Arts Archives, Vienna/Uffizi, Florence. **88:** Scala, Flor-

ence. **89:** Scala, Florence—Scala/Art Resource, N.Y. **90:** Giraudon, Paris. **91:** Scala, Florence—Plessner/Schapowalow, Hamburg/National Gallery, London. **92:** Alinari-Giraudon, Paris—Ancient Art and Architecture Collection, Pinner, Middlesex, England. **93:** Library of Congress; William Albert Allard, © National Geographic Image Collection. **94, 95:** Alinari-Giraudon, Paris; Scala, Florence. **97:** Photo RMN, Paris—Palazzo Vecchio, Florence/ Bridgeman Art Library, London. **98:** Erich Lessing Culture and Fine Arts Archives, Vienna/Palazzo Schifanoia, Ferrara, Italy—AKG, Berlin/Orsi Battaglini/Museo Firenze com' era. **101:** Erich Lessing Culture and Fine Arts Archives, Vienna/ House of Machiavelli, Percussina, Italy. **103:** Scala, Florence. **104:** Cameraphoto, Venice. **105:** Artephot/Oronoz. **106, 107:** Scala, Florence; © The Cleveland Museum of Art, Holden Collection, 1916.801—*The Youthful David,* Widener Collection, © 1998 Board of Trustees, National Gallery of Art, Washington, D.C. **108:** Alinari-Giraudon, Paris. **109:** Erich Lessing Culture and Fine Arts Archives, Vienna/Banca Monte dei Paschi, Siena, Italy. **110, 111:** Beinecke Rare Book and Manuscript Library, Yale University; frontispiece from *Canzone per Andare in Màschera per Carnesciale,* by Lorenzo de' Medici and others, woodcut after 1497, Biblioteca Nazionale Centrale, Florence—© Isabella Stewart Gardner Museum, Boston. **112, 113:** Scala, Florence; Alinari/Art Resource, N.Y. **115:** Art Resource, N.Y. **116:** Erich Lessing Culture and Fine Arts Archives, Vienna/Santa Maria Novella, Florence. **118:** Biblioteca Estense Universitaria, Modena/ET Archive, London. **119:** Naval Museum, Genoa/ET Archive, London. **120, 121:** Dimitri Kessel. **122, 123:** Ted Speigel, © National Geographic Image Collection. **125:** Photo Hubert Josse, Paris. **126:** Scala, Florence—AKG, Paris; Galleria dell'Accadèmia, Venice/Bridgeman Art Library, London—Scala, Florence. **127:** Biblioteca Ambrosiana, Milan—Giraudon, Paris—Biblioteca Ambrosiana, Milan. **128:** Erich Lessing Culture and Fine Arts Archives, Vienna/Galleria Nazionale di Capodimonte, Naples, Italy. **130:** Erich Lessing Culture and Fine Arts Archives, Vienna/National Gallery, London. **132:** The British Library, London. **134:** Erich Lessing Culture and Fine Arts Archives, Vienna/Santa Maria Novella, Florence. **135:** Scala, Florence; Erich Lessing Culture and Fine Arts Archives, Vienna/Villa Rotonda, Vicenza, Italy. **136:** Erich Lessing Culture and Fine Arts Archives, Vienna/Santa Maria Novella, Florence—Scala, Florence.

137: Photo RMN–R. G. Ojeda. **139:** Scala/Art Resource, N.Y. **141:** Ted Speigel, © National Geographic Image Collection. **143:** AKG, Berlin/Staatliches Lindenau-Museum, Altenburg; Scala, Florence—AKG, Berlin/Erich Lessing/Muzeum Zamek W Lancucie, Lancut, Poland. **145:** Scala, Florence; Scala/Art Resource, N.Y. **146, 147:** Musei Vaticani, Rome; Michelangelo—Poem and sketch of the artist at work on the ceiling of the Sistine Chapel, courtesy Casa Buonarroti, Florence.

149-157: Background by John Drummond, © Time Life Inc., marble courtesy *Ademas*, Alexandria, Va. **149:** Dan Budnick/Woodfin Camp. **150:** The British Library, London—from *Le Basiliche Cristiane, Dissertazioni Lette nell'Accadèmia Pontificia di Archeologia negli Anni 1891-1892,* published Rome, 1892. By Monsignor Pietro Crostarosa, courtesy Biblioteca Hertziana, Rome. **151:** Louvre, Paris/ET Archive, London. **152, 153:** Civiche Raccolte Archeologiche e Numismatiche, Milan. Cat. No.

284; Luciano Romano—FMR, Milan; Kupferstichkabinett, Staatliche Museen zu Berlin-Preussischer Kulturbesitz. **154, 155:** Scala, Florence; Mario Quattrone/Gabinetto Disegni, Uffizi, Florence; Biblioteca Apostolica Vaticana, Rome. **156, 157:** Ancient Art and Architecture Collection, Pinner, Middlesex, England; Scala, Florence.

Design Elements: The Board of Trinity College Dublin, Dublin, Ireland.

BIBLIOGRAPHY

BOOKS

Alexander, Jonathan J. G., ed. *The Painted Page: Italian Renaissance Book Illumination, 1450-1550.* London: Royal Academy of Arts, 1994.

Atchity, Kenneth J., ed. *The Renaissance Reader.* New York: HarperPerennial, 1996.

Bernier, Olivier. *The Renaissance Princes.* Chicago: Stonehenge, 1983.

Bertelli, Sergio, Franco Cardini, and Elvira Garbero Zorzi. *The Courts of the Italian Renaissance.* New York: Facts on File, 1986.

Birbari, Elizabeth. *Dress in Italian Painting, 1460-1500.* London: John Murray, 1975.

Black, C., et al. *Renaissance.* Chicago: Stonehenge, 1993.

Bramly, Serge. *Leonardo: Discovering the Life of Leonardo da Vinci.* Trans. by Stan Reynolds. New York: Edward Burlingame Books, 1991.

Breisach, Ernst. *Caterina Sforza.* Chicago: University of Chicago Press, 1967.

Brown, Patricia Fortini:
Art and Life in Renaissance Venice. New York: Harry N. Abrams, 1997.
Venetian Narrative Painting in the Age of Carpaccio. New Haven, Conn.: Yale University Press, 1988.

Brucker, Gene A.:
Florence: The Golden Age, 1138-1737. Berkeley: University of California Press, 1983.
Giovanni and Lusanna: Love and Marriage in Renaissance Florence. Berkeley: University of California Press, 1986.
Renaissance Florence. Berkeley: University of California Press, 1983.

Bull, George. *Michelangelo: A Biography.* New York: St. Martin's Press, 1995.

Burckhardt, Jacob. *The Civilization of the Renaissance in Italy* (Vol. 1). New York: Harper & Row, 1958.

Burke, James. *The Day the Universe Changed.*

Boston: Little, Brown, 1985.

Burke, Peter. *Culture and Society in Renaissance Italy, 1420-1540.* New York: Charles Scribner's Sons, 1972.

Cecchi, Alessandro. *The Piccolomini Library in the Cathedral of Siena.* Florence: Scala, 1982.

Chamberlin, E. R. *The Bad Popes.* New York: Dial Press, 1969.

Christiansen, Keith. *Andrea Mantegna, Padua and Mantua.* New York: George Braziller, 1994.

Clark, Kenneth. *Leonardo da Vinci: His Account of His Development as an Artist.* Baltimore: Penguin Books, 1958.

Cole, Alison. *Virtue and Magnificence: Art of the Italian Renaissance Courts.* New York: Harry N. Abrams, 1995.

Columbia Encyclopedia. New York: Columbia University Press, 1979.

Davies, Martin. *Aldus Manutius: Printer and Publisher of Renaissance Venice.* Malibu, Calif.: J. Paul Getty Museum, 1995.

De Grazia, Sebastian. *Machiavelli in Hell.* Princeton, N.J.: Princeton University Press, 1989.

De Mause, Lloyd, ed. *The History of Childhood.* New York: Psychohistory Press, 1974.

Di Stefano, Roberto. *La Cupola di San Pietro.* Naples: Edizioni Scientifiche Italiane, 1980.

Durant, Will. *The Renaissance: A History of Civilization in Italy from 1304-1576 A.D.* New York: Simon and Schuster, 1953.

Florence, Italie. Paris: Guides Gallimard, n.d.

Francia, Ennio. *Storia Della Costruzione del Nuovo San Pietro.* Rome: De Luca, 1989.

Gage, John. *Life in Italy: At the Time of the Medici.* London: B. T. Batsford, 1968.

Garin, Eugenio. *Portraits from the Quattrocento.* Trans. by Victor A. Velen and Elizabeth Velen. New York: Harper & Row, 1963.

Gasponi, Giancarlo. *Umbria: Land of Harmony.* Trento, Italy: Euroedit, 1995.

Grendler, Paul F. *Schooling in Renaissance Italy: Liter-*

acy and Learning, 1300-1600. Baltimore: Johns Hopkins University Press, 1989.

Guedj, Denis. *Numbers: The Universal Language.* London: Thames and Hudson, 1996.

Hale, J. R. *Florence and the Medici: The Pattern of Control.* London: Thames and Hudson, 1977.

Hale, John R., and the Editors of Time-Life Books:
Age of Exploration (Great Ages of Man series). New York: Time-Life Books, 1966.
Renaissance (Great Ages of Man series). New York: Time-Life Books, 1965.

Hammond, Inc.:
Historical Atlas of the World. Maplewood, N.J.: Hammond, 1984.
The Times Atlas of World History. Ed. by Geoffrey Barraclough. Maplewood, N.J.: Hammond, 1993.

Hay, Denys, ed. *The Age of the Renaissance.* London: Thames and Hudson, 1986.

Herald, Jacqueline. *Renaissance Dress in Italy, 1400-1500* (History of Dress series). London: Bell & Hyman, 1981.

Hersey, George L. *High Renaissance Art in St. Peter's and the Vatican: An Interpretive Guide.* Chicago: University of Chicago Press, 1993.

Hibbert, Christopher:
The House of Medici: Its Rise and Fall. New York: Morrow Quill, 1980.
The Popes. Chicago: Stonehenge, 1982.

The Holy Bible. New York: Thomas Nelson & Sons, 1952.

The Horizon Book of the Renaissance. New York: American Heritage, 1961.

Hughes, Graham. *Renaissance Cassoni: Masterpieces of Early Italian Art: Painted Marriage Chests, 1400-1550.* Sussex, England: Starcity, 1997.

Jardine, Lisa. *Worldly Goods: A New History of the Renaissance.* New York: Doubleday, 1996.

Jestaz, Bertrand. *Architecture of the Renaissance: From Brunelleschi to Palladio.* London: Thames and Hudson, 1996.

Jung-Inglessis, E. M. *St. Peter's.* Florence: Scala, 1980.

Kemp, Martin. *Leonardo da Vinci: The Marvelous Works of Nature and Man.* Cambridge, Mass.: Harvard University Press, 1981.

King, Margaret L. *Women of the Renaissance.* Chicago: University of Chicago Press, 1991.

Klapisch-Zuber, Christiane. *Women, Family, and Ritual in Renaissance Italy.* Trans. by Lydia Cochrane. Chicago: University of Chicago Press, 1985.

Landucci, Luca. *A Florentine Diary: From 1450-1516.* Trans. by Alice De Rosen Jervis. Freeport, N.Y.: Books for Libraries Press, 1971 (reprint of 1927 edition).

Lane, Frederic C. *Venice: A Maritime Republic.* Baltimore: Johns Hopkins University Press, 1973.

Lees-Milne, James. *Saint Peter's: The Story of Saint Peter's Basilica in Rome.* Boston: Little, Brown, 1967.

Lightbrown, Ronald. *Sandro Botticelli: Life and Work.* New York: Abbeville Press, 1989.

Lucas-Dubreton, J. *Daily Life in Florence: In the Time of the Medici.* Trans. by A. Lytton Sells. New York: Macmillan, 1961.

McBrien, Richard P. *Lives of the Popes: The Pontiffs from St. Peter to John Paul II.* New York: HarperCollins, 1997.

Machiavelli, Niccolò. *The Prince.* Trans. by George Bull. Baltimore: Penguin Books, 1961.

Macinghi Strozzi, Alessandra. *Selected Letters of Alessandra Strozzi.* Trans. by Heather Gregory. Berkeley: University of California Press, 1997.

Maxwell-Stuart, P. G. *Chronicle of the Popes.* London: Thames and Hudson, 1997.

Menen, Aubrey. *Upon This Rock.* New York: Saturday Review Press, 1972.

Michelangelo. *Complete Poems and Selected Letters of Michelangelo.* Ed. by Robert N. Linscott, trans. by Creighton Gilbert. Princeton, N.J.: Princeton University Press, 1980.

Muir, Edward. *Civic Ritual in Renaissance Venice.* Princeton, N.J.: Princeton University Press, 1981.

Murray, Linda. *Michelangelo: His Life, Work and Times.* London: Thames and Hudson, 1984.

Murray, Peter, and Linda Murray. *A Dictionary of Art and Artists.* Baltimore: Penguin Books, 1972.

National Gallery: Washington (Great Museums of the World series). Milan: Arnoldo Mondadori Editore, 1968.

National Geographic Atlas of the World. Washington, D.C.: National Geographic Society, 1970.

Origo, Iris. *The Merchant of Prato.* New York: Alfred A. Knopf, 1957.

Paglia, J. *What to See in Rome and Environs.* Rome: Giovanni Lanza, 1950.

The Panorama of the Renaissance. Ed. by Margaret Aston. New York: Harry N. Abrams, 1996.

Paoletti, John T., and Gary M. Radke. *Art in Renaissance Italy.* Upper Saddle River, N.J.: Prentice Hall, 1997.

Plumb, J. H. *Renaissance Profiles.* New York: Harper & Row, 1965.

Pierpont Morgan Library. *In August Company.* New York: Pierpont Morgan Library, 1993.

Pope-Hennessy, John, and Keith Christiansen. *Secular Painting in 15th-Century Tuscany: Birth Trays, Cassone Panels, and Portraits.* New York: Metropolitan Museum of Art, 1980.

Raggio, Olga, and Antoine M. Wilmering. *The Liberal Arts Studiolo from the Ducal Palace at Gubbio.* New York: Metropolitan Museum of Art, 1996.

Reader's Digest. *Everyday Life through the Ages.* London: Reader's Digest, 1992.

The Renaissance (The Cultural Atlas of the World series). Alexandria, Va.: Stonehenge, 1993.

Renaissance Characters. Ed. by Eugenio Garin, trans. by Lydia G. Cochrane. Chicago: University of Chicago Press, 1991.

The Renaissance: Maker of Modern Man. [Washington]: National Geographic Society, 1977.

The Roots of Western Civilization: Man on the Move. Danbury, Conn.: Grolier Educational, 1994.

Rosenberg, Louis Conrad. *The Davanzati Palace, Florence Italy.* New York: Architectural Book Publishing, 1922.

Schneider, Norbert. *The Art of the Portrait: Masterpieces of European Portrait-Painting, 1420-1670.* N.p.: Barnes & Noble, 1994.

Strocchia, Sharon T. *Death and Ritual in Renaissance Florence.* Baltimore: Johns Hopkins University Press, 1992.

Strong, Roy. *Art and Power: Renaissance Festivals, 1450-1650.* Woodbridge, Suffolk, England: Boydell Press, 1984.

Thompson, Bard. *Humanists and Reformers: A History of the Renaissance and Reformation.* Grand Rapids: William B. Eerdmans, 1996.

Thubron, Colin, and the Editors of Time-Life Books. *The Venetians* (The Seafarers series). Alexandria, Va.: Time-Life Books, 1980.

The Times Atlas of the World. New York: Times Books, 1980.

Tinagli, Paola. *Women in Italian Renaissance Art.* Manchester, England: Manchester University Press, 1997.

Trexler, Richard C. *Public Life in Renaissance Florence.* New York: Academic Press, 1980.

Turner, A. Richard. *Renaissance Florence: The Invention of a New Art.* New York: Harry N. Abrams, 1997.

Vasari, Giorgio. *The Great Masters.* Ed. by Michael Sonino, trans. by Gaston Du C. de Vere. New York: Macmillan, 1986.

Venise, Italie. Paris: Guides Gallimard, n.d.

Vezzosi, Alessandro. *Leonardo da Vinci: Renaissance Man.* London: Thames and Hudson, 1996.

Voyages of Discovery: TimeFrame AD 1400-1500 (Time Frame series). Alexandria, Va.: Time-Life Books, 1989.

Wallace, Robert, and the Editors of Time-Life Books. *The World of Leonardo, 1452-1519* (Time-Life Library of Art series). New York: Time, 1966.

Welch, Evelyn. *Art and Society in Italy, 1350-1500.* Oxford, England: Oxford University Press, 1997.

PERIODICALS

Firenze, April 1996.

King, Margaret L. "The Religious Retreat of Isotta Nogarola (1418-1466): Sexism and Its Consequences in the Fifteenth Century." *Signs: Journal of Women in Culture and Society,* Summer 1978.

"Triumphal Celebrations and the Rituals of Statecraft." Part 1 of *Papers in Art History from the Pennsylvania State University,* 1990, Vol. 6.

OTHER SOURCES

Italian Renaissance Architecture. Exhibition catalog. Washington, D.C.: National Gallery of Art, 1994.

Leonardo da Vinci: Scientist, Inventor, Artist. Exhibition catalog. Tübingen, Germany: Institut Für Kulturaustausch, 1997.

Millon, Henry A., and Craig Hugh Smyth. *Michelangelo, Architect.* Exhibition catalog. Washington, D.C.: National Gallery of Art, October 9-December 11, 1988.

INDEX

Numerals in italics indicate an illustration of the subject mentioned.

Philosophy: Christian Platonism, 114; humanism, 10, 114-115, 135

Piazza della Signoria: Savonarola's execution in, *94-95*

Pico della Mirandola, Giovanni: 10, *115*, 119, 137; academic background of, 113-114; and Margherita, 115-116; and Platonic Academy, 114-115

Pietà: 133, 137, *139*

Pinturicchio: painting by, *18*

Pisa: 77, 86, 96; trade with Near East, 9

Pistoia: 45

Pius II (pope): 21, 24, *82,* 83; ring of, *81*

Platina: *82*

Platonic Academy: 9, 114-115; members of, *116*

Politics: and arranged marriages, 15

Poliziano, Angelo: 114, *116,* 137

Pollaiuolo, Antonio: 137

Portrait of a Man and a Woman at a Casement: 26

Prince, The: 11, 19, 99-102

Printing: italic typeface, 132; presses in Italy, 9, 132

Pucci family: 38

Pulci, Luigi: 114

R

Raphael: 82, 150, 152; painting by, *112-113*

Reformation: 83

Reggio: 21

Renaissance: 8; moves beyond Italy, 11; secular and economic transitions in, 11

Resurrection, The: 18

Riario, Cardinal Raffaele: 71, 72, 78-79

Rizzoni, Martino: 54, 57

Romagna: 100

Rome: *81,* 117, 150; and Borgias, 19, 133-134; classical legacy of, 8; government of, 9, 15; refurbished by popes, 80-83; sacked by troops of

Holy Roman Empire, 11; University of, 19

Rucellai, Marietta: 51, 54

Rucellai, Piero di Cardinale: 51

S

St. Peter's basilica: 83, 139, *149, 155;* construction of, 152, *153, 154,* 155; designs for, *152-153,* 154; inner dome of, *156-157;* nave, *156;* original basilica at, *150*

Salai, Giacomo: 127-129, 131

Salviati, Alamanno: 130

Salviati, Francesco: 77, 78, 79, 80

Salviati family: 77

Sangallo, Antonio da: 152, 155; design for St. Peter's, *152-153*

San Marco (church): 85, 89, 94, 118

San Piero a Pitiana: 49-51

San Romano, Battle of: *130*

San Sebastiano (church): 23

Santa Maria delle Grazie (monastery): 119-122

Santa Maria Novella (church): *134*

Sant'Andrea (church): 23

Santissima Annunziata (church): 41, 52; tabernacle at, *53*

Santo Spirito (church): *135*

Savonarola, Girolamo: 88-90, *95,* 100, 118; execution of, 10, *94-95;* and Lorenzo de' Medici, 85

Scala, Alessandra: 59

School of Athens: 112-113

School of princes: 15, 23

Science: classical influence on, 10

Sculpture: classical influence on, 10

Sforza, Alessandro: 17

Sforza, Battista: *17*

Sforza, Caterina: 100, 142, *143*

Sforza, Francesco: *24*

Sforza, Galeazzo: 24

Sforza, Ludovico: 24, *25,* 119, 120, 122

Sforza, Massimiliano: tutoring of, *56*

Sforza family: and Milan, 13, 24, 125

Shakespeare, William: 11

Shoes: platform design of, *64*

Siena: 80; festivals, *108, 109;* government of, 9; patron saint of, 108

Signoria: 76, 86, 88, 94, 142

Sistine Chapel: 83, 142-144; Michelangelo's ceiling at, *146-147*

Sixtus IV (pope): 9, 71, 76-77, 80, *82,* 83, 93

Soderini, Piero: 96, 142

Sorbonne: 113, 118

Spanish Inquisition: 9, 83

Strozzi, Alessandra: 27-32, 35-37, 39-42, 46

Strozzi, Alfonso: 42, 46

Strozzi, Caterina: 35-37, 39

Strozzi, Filippo: 27, 29, *30,* 31, 32, 39, 41, 42, 46

Strozzi, Lessandra: 39

Strozzi, Lorenzo: 27, 29, 41

Strozzi, Matteo (father): 28

Strozzi, Matteo (son): 27, 39

Strozzi, Tito Vespasiano: 21

Strozzi family: 27-46

Subiaco: 9

Summa di Arithmetica: 129

T

Tanagli family: 42

Taxes: 32

Theologia Platonica: 114

Theology: and humanism, 10

Tolentino, Niccolò da: 130

Torquemada: 118

Torrigiano, Pietro: 140

Trieste: 92

Tura, Cosimo: 21

Tuscany: 10; olive groves and grape arbors in, *98*

U

Ubertini, Francesco: painting by, *43*

Uccello, Paolo: 136

Universities: 19, 21, 59, 113, 114, 118

Urban VIII: 155

Urbino: 19; and Federigo da Montefeltro, 17; government of, 15; library at, 17

V

Veneto: 91

Venice: 21, 24, 58, 64, 77, 83, *91,* 124, 129, 132; beautification of, 92; festivals, *105, 110,* 111; galleys, *92;* and glassblowing industry, *93;* government of, 9; Grand Canal and the Rialto, *90, 91;* population of, 8-9; shipyard in, *92;* trading empire of, 9, 91-92

Vernet, Horace: 150

Verona: 54, 56, 58, 92

Verrocchio, Andrea del: 124; bust by, *70*

Vespasiano da Bisticci: 17

Vespucci, Simonetta: 50

Villa di Collesalvetti: *98*

Villa Rotondo: *135*

Vinci: *122-123,* 124

Virgin and Child with Saint Anne, The: 131

Virgin Annunciate: 61

Virgin of the Rocks: 120

Visconti, Bianca Maria: *24*

Visconti, Filippo Maria: 24

W

Warfare: condottieres, 17; mercenaries, 130

Weaving: loom, *29*

Women: chaperons for, 32, 42; and childbirth, 40, 53; education of, 56, 57-59; fashions in clothing, *64, 65;* hair styles, 66, *67;* ideal of beauty, 50; new roles for, 142; religious devotions of, 61; traditional life for, 142

Z

Ziani, Sebastiano: *104*

TIME® LIFE BOOKS

Time-Life Books is a division of Time Life Inc.

TIME LIFE INC.
PRESIDENT and CEO: George Artandi

TIME-LIFE BOOKS
PUBLISHER/MANAGING EDITOR: Neil Kagan
VICE PRESIDENT, MARKETING: Joseph A. Kuna
VICE PRESIDENT, NEW PRODUCT
DEVELOPMENT: Amy Golden

What Life Was Like
AT THE REBIRTH OF GENIUS

EDITOR: Denise Dersin
DIRECTOR, NEW PRODUCT DEVELOPMENT:
Elizabeth D. Ward
DIRECTOR OF MARKETING: Pamela R. Farrell

Deputy Editor: Paula York-Soderlund
Design Director: Cynthia T. Richardson
Text Editor: Robin Currie
Associate Editor/Research and Writing:
Trudy W. Pearson
Senior Copyeditor: Mary Beth Oelkers-Keegan
Technical Art Specialist: John Drummond
Picture Coordinator: David Herod
Editorial Assistant: Christine Higgins

Special Contributors: Ronald H. Bailey, Ellen Galford,
Dónal Kevin Gordon (chapter text); Gaye Brown, Jane
Coughran, Sarah L. Evans, Christina Huth, Marilyn
Murphy Terrell, Elizabeth Thompson (research-writing);
Meghan K. Blute, Jessica K. Ferrell, Beth Levin (research);
Janet Cave (editing); Lina Baber Burton (glossary); Roy
Nanovic (index); Barbara L. Klein (overread).

Correspondents: Christine Hinze (London), Christina
Lieberman (New York), Maria Vincenza Aloisi (Paris).
Valuable assistance was also provided by Elizabeth
Kraemer-Singh, Angelika Lemmer (Bonn), Ann Natanson
(Rome).

Director of Finance: Christopher Hearing
Directors of Book Production: Marjann Caldwell,
Patricia Pascale
Director of Publishing Technology: Betsi McGrath
Director of Photography and Research: John Conrad Weiser
Director of Editorial Administration: Barbara Levitt
Manager, Technical Services: Anne Topp
Senior Production Manager: Ken Sabol
Production Manager: Virginia Reardon
Quality Assurance Manager: James King
Chief Librarian: Louise D. Forstall

Consultant:
Richard Stapleford received his Ph.D. from the Institute
of Fine Arts of New York University and is a Fellow of
the American Academy in Rome. He is a professor of art
history at Hunter College of the City University of New
York, where he teaches a wide range of courses in both
medieval and Renaissance art. His publications include
articles on Botticelli and Vasari as well as on medieval
and Renaissance architecture. Dr. Stapleford is currently
completing a translation of the inventory of the estate of
Lorenzo de' Medici and a monograph on Botticelli.

First printing. Printed in U.S.A.
School and library distribution by Time-Life Education,
P.O. Box 85026, Richmond, Virginia 23285-5026.

TIME-LIFE is a trademark of Time Warner Inc. U.S.A.

Library of Congress Cataloging-in-Publication Data
What life was like at the rebirth of genius : Renaissance
Italy, AD 1400-1550 / by the editors of Time-Life Books.
     p.   cm.—(What life was like ; 12)
    Includes bibliographical references and index.
    ISBN 0-7835-5461-3
    1. Renaissance—Italy. 2. Italy—Civilization—
1268-1559.
I. Title. II. Series: What life was like series ; 12.
DG445.T56 1999   99-10635
945'.05—dc21   CIP

This volume is one in a series on world history that
uses contemporary art, artifacts, and personal accounts
to create an intimate portrait of daily life in the past.

Other volumes included in the
What Life Was Like series:

Other Publications:
HISTORY
Our American Century
World War II
The American Story
Voices of the Civil War
The American Indians
Lost Civilizations
Mysteries of the Unknown
Time Frame
The Civil War
Cultural Atlas

COOKING
Weight Watchers® Smart Choice Recipe Collection
Great Taste~Low Fat
Williams-Sonoma Kitchen Library

SCIENCE/NATURE
Voyage Through the Universe

DO IT YOURSELF
Total Golf
How to Fix It
The Time-Life Complete Gardener
Home Repair and Improvement
The Art of Woodworking

TIME-LIFE KIDS
Student Library
Library of First Questions and Answers
A Child's First Library of Learning
I Love Math
Nature Company Discoveries
Understanding Science & Nature

For information on and a full description of any of the
Time-Life Books series listed above, please call 1-800-
621-7026 or write:

Reader Information
Time-Life Customer Service
P.O. Box C-32068
Richmond, Virginia 23261-2068